CHICAGO · BLACKHAWKS · STANLEY CUP CHAMPIONS

HOCKEY NOW!

EIGHTH EDITION

MIKE LEONETTI

FIREFLY BOOKS

A FIREFLY BOOK

Published by Firefly Books Ltd. 2015

First printing

Publisher Cataloging-in-Publication Data (U.S.)
Leonetti, Mike, 1958-
    Hockey Now! : the biggest stars of the NHL / Mike Leonetti.
8th edition.
[160] pages : color photographs ; cm.
Includes index.
Summary: "Illustrated profiles with more than 130 colorful action photos of star
players in the National Hockey League"– Provided by publisher.
ISBN-13: 978-1-77085-600-4 (pbk.)
1. National Hockey League – Pictorial works. 2. National Hockey League –
Biography. I. Title.
796.962/0922 dc23   GV848.5.L467 2015

Library and Archives Canada Cataloguing in Publication
Leonetti, Mike, 1958-, author
        Hockey now! : the biggest stars of the NHL / Mike Leonetti. --
Eighth edition.
Includes index.
ISBN 978-1-77085-600-4 (paperback)
1. Hockey players--Biography. 2. National Hockey League. 3. Hockey players-
-Pictorial works. 4. National Hockey League--Pictorial works. I. Title.
GV848.5.A1L455 2015   796.962092'2   C2015-905018-9

Published in the United States by
Firefly Books (U.S.) Inc.
P.O. Box 1338, Ellicott Station
Buffalo, New York 14205

Published in Canada in 2015 by
Firefly Books Ltd.
50 Staples Avenue, Unit 1
Richmond Hill, Ontario L4B 0A7

Cover and interior design: Kimberley Young

Printed in Canada

The publisher gratefully acknowledges the financial support for our publishing
program by the Government of Canada through the Canada Book Fund as
administered by the Department of Canadian Heritage.

PHOTO CREDITS

Icon Sportswire:

Robin Alam: 1, 8, 44, 49, 50, 68, 75, 84, 98, 108, 124, 125; Steven
Alkok: 55; Gavin Baker: 145; Justin Berl: 95, 100; John Cordes: 141;
Jerome Davis: 47, 138; Ted Davis: 121; Andrew Dieb: 117; Brian
Ekart: 26, 109; Bob Frid: 51, 66, 83, 153; Keith Gillett: 13, 36, 104;
Mark Goldman: 19, 39, 115; Rich Graessle: 12, 14, 16, 22, 23, 35,
54, 56, 130, 152, 156; Scott W. Grau: 3, 17, 137; Dan Hamilton: 30, 158, 159; Derik Hamilton: 31,
78; John Hefti: 63, 67, 93, 119; Kathleen Hinkel: 46; Fred Kfoury
III: 9, 29, 107, 129; Steven King: 37; Jason Kopinski: 85; Russell
Lansford: 24, 120, 157; Tommy LaPorte: 126; Tim Larson: 34, 82;
Terrence Lee: 69, 103; Jeanine Leech: 15, 28, 32, 33, 38, 48, 53, 61,
62, 64, 74, 76, 77, 86, 96, 99, 112, 114, 122, 132, 133, 134, 136,
144; Mark LoMoglio: 10, 42, 45, 52, 73, 97, 148, 154; Jason Mowry:
81; Danny Murphy: 60, 89, 149; Minas Panagiotakis: 20, 21, 43, 72,
106, 116, 127, 139, 142, 143, 150, 151, 155; Brad Rempel: 25, 58,
59, 79, 88, 118, 131; Marc Sanchez: 4–5; Leslie Schiff: 11; Jimmy
Simmons: 65, 113; Ric Tapia: 140; Greg Thompson: 135; Nick
Turchiaro: 102; Michael Tureski: 87, 94; Chris Williams: 57, 92,
105, 128

Front Cover:
Robin Alam (Toews); Rich Graessle (Suter); Jeanine Leech (Crosby
and Stamkos); Jason Mowry (Nash)

Back Cover:
Robin Alam (top); Danny Murphy (Weber); Minas Panagiotakis
(Price)

DEDICATION

The eighth edition of *Hockey Now!* is dedicated to all
the members of the Chicago Blackhawks organization
who have won three Stanley Cups in the last six years,
including 2015. A special salute to head coach Joel
Quenneville, who was behind the Chicago bench for
all three championships.

TI·AYD·346

CONTENTS

INTRODUCTION

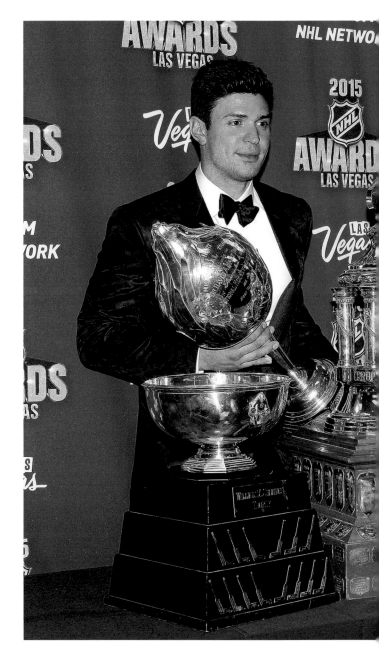

When Montreal Canadiens goaltender Carey Price was named the winner of the Hart Memorial Trophy as the most valuable player in the NHL for the 2014–15 season, it provided a fitting end to the "Year of the Goaltender." Price, who also won the William M. Jennings Trophy, the Ted Lindsay Award and the Vezina Trophy, was by far the best player on his team and set a franchise record with 44 wins while compiling a 1.96 goals-against average and a save percentage of .933. These numbers indicate just how much Price dominated over the entire season, but he was not the only netminder to have a great year.

Goaltenders Pekka Rinne of the Nashville Predators, Braden Holtby of the Washington Capitals and Ben Bishop of the Tampa Bay Lightning also won 40 or more games each. Veteran Marc-Andre Fleury of the Pittsburgh Penguins led the league with 10 shutouts, while Jonathan Quick of the Los Angeles Kings, Tuukka Rask of the Boston Bruins and Cory Schneider of the New Jersey Devils all played 69 or more games, giving their teams a chance to win night after night. Most modern goaltenders — with these aforementioned netminders being no exception — are large men who block out a major portion of the net based on their size alone, but they are also athletic, durable and wear their large equipment with ease. It's no surprise, then, that the crease-keepers rule today's NHL game.

In 2014–15, the league averaged 5.33 goals per game and no player recorded more than 87 points, with Jamie Benn of the Dallas Stars taking the Art Ross Trophy (the last time the point-total was less than 100 in a full 82-game season was 2003–04). The only other players to record over 80 points were John Tavares (86), Sidney Crosby (84), Alex Ovechkin (81) and Jakub

Voracek (81). Only Ovechkin scored over 50 goals (53), and while Steven Stamkos and Rick Nash each had over 40, only 15 players scored 30 or more markers.

These small scoring numbers continued into the play-offs when one-goal games occurred on a regular basis. Further, the Stanley Cup finals produced a total of only 23 goals in six games. There wasn't too much room on the ice for free-wheeling offensive plays, and third– and fourth-line players were often solely dedicated to stopping

some of the best two-way defensemen in the history of the game are becoming more prominent. Duncan Keith, Shea Weber, Drew Doughty, Ryan Suter, P.K. Subban, Erik Karlsson, Alex Pietrangelo, Mark Giordano, Victor Hedman and Brent Burns are but a few of the dominating blue-liners that add great excitement to the game when they defend or attack. No team can win without at least one of these offense-oriented defensemen who can get the puck out of their own end before leading the rush into the opposition's zone.

It's also positive to see so many good young players making their mark in the league, such as Aaron Ekblad, Johnny Gaudreau, Tyler Johnson, Morgan Rielly, Nathan MacKinnon, Filip Forsberg and Alex Galchenyuk. Newcomers to watch in 2015–16 include Connor McDavid and Jack Eichel — two offensive dynamos who are sure to challenge the goals-against average of all NHL netminders.

Considering that both teams in the 2015 Stanley Cup final had incredible offensive and defensive numbers in the regular season (the Chicago Blackhawks tied for the fewest goals allowed and the Tampa Bay Lightning scored the most), it's likely that goaltending will remain prominent in 2015–16 as teams try and emulate the most successful clubs. By taking three championships in six seasons in the age of the salary cap, Chicago has also proven that a dynasty is still possible.

The eighth edition of *Hockey Now!* has updated the profiles of the players who appeared in the previous version, and it contains many new additions as well. All of the players mentioned in this introduction (excluding McDavid and Eichel) are profiled, plus many more of the most exciting hockey players in the NHL today. Whether you want to read about leaders like Jonathan Toews, shot blockers like Ryan McDonagh or goal scorers like Phil Kessel, this book profiles them all.

I hope you enjoy my look at the game today with this latest version of *Hockey Now!*

the opposition from scoring. The salary cap has also imposed parity among the 30 teams in the league because no one can keep a lot of offensive players together — they simply cost too much. More shots on goal may be the only thing that will help the attackers' cause because goalies are not going to get smaller, nor is their equipment likely to shrink by any significant amount.

One of the better aspects of the current NHL is that

Mike Leonetti

EASTERN CONFERENCE TEAM STARS

The best of the Atlantic and Metropolitan Divisions.

Rick NASH
LEFT WING 61

Roberto JONGO

Cory
SCHNEIDER

GOALTENDER
35

CENTER
91

Patri
BERG

Claude
GIROUX

CENTER
28

Carey

GOALTENDER

Eastern Conference Team Star

Patrice **BERGERON**

CENTER **37**

that the native of L'Ancienne-Lorette, Quebec, is "what every coach dreams of in a player," and that Bergeron is an elite performer at both ends of the rink. Not many players receive such public acclaim from their coaches, indicating that Bergeron has had nothing but a positive effect in his 11 seasons with the Bruins.

Bergeron has already won a few major NHL awards; he received the Frank J. Selke Trophy (which recognizes the best defensive forward) on three occasions, the most recent coming for his performance in the 2014–15 season. Bergeron recorded 55 points (23 goals and 32 assists) and raised his career plus/minus total to plus-110, which puts him in the top 20 active players with the best plus/minus records. Bergeron became the first Bruin to win the Selke consecutively and is now tied with Pavel Datsyuk, the only other active player with more than two.

Bergeron's attention to defense means he is unlikely to put up big scoring numbers, but his average of about 60 points over the last five seasons is certainly respectable. A major part of Bergeron's game is taking faceoffs, especially in his own zone. In 2014–15, he took the most faceoffs in the league (1,951) and had the best percentage (60.2%), proving he could handle his new role as the primary faceoff-taker for his team after an injury to teammate and faceoff regular David Krejci.

Bergeron's game is more than just his skill as a defensive forward or faceoff man. He is a threat to score at any point and can set up a teammate nicely (he has been in the top 3 in assists on the Bruins team since 2009–10). And even though the Bruins didn't make the playoffs at the end of their 2014–15 campaign, Bergeron kept his team in contention right up until the end of the regular season.

When the Toronto Maple Leafs rolled into Boston on April 4, 2015, the Bruins were holding the second wild-card spot in the Eastern Conference. Bergeron

P atrice Bergeron is one of the most complete players in the NHL and the Boston Bruins would not have it any other way. Few players can compete at Bergeron's level, playing two-way hockey year in and year out. His courage and leadership were especially noted when he played in the 2013 playoffs with a broken rib, torn cartilage and a bad shoulder. It is therefore no wonder that the 6-foot-2, 194-pound center was the Bruins' nominee for the 2015 Bill Masterton Memorial Trophy, which recognizes sportsmanship, perseverance and dedication to hockey.

Boston coach Claude Julien was lavish in his praise of Bergeron when the nomination was announced, telling those gathered that his best forward was a dedicated player both on and off the ice. Julien stated

scored the only Boston goal in regulation time and then added the only marker of the shoot-out to give his team a 2–1 victory. The win gave the Bruins a leg up on the encroaching Ottawa Senators, but three consecutive losses sealed the Bruins' fate and they missed the post-season for the first time in eight years.

Changes to the Bruins' organization began soon after the elimination from the playoffs as general manager Peter Chiarelli was fired. This was nothing new for Bergeron, who had seen many come and go in Boston. He was there when superstar center Joe Thornton was traded and watched while coaches like Mike Sullivan and Dave Lewis were replaced. Throughout this upheaval, the talented center has

remained a steadying influence on the team and became an important part of Boston's Stanley Cup win in 2011. Bergeron scored a key goal in the final game of the series against the Vancouver Canucks while totaling 20 points in 23 playoff games.

As the Bruins continue to tinker with the lineup in an attempt to keep pace with the high scoring clubs in the Eastern Conference, fans can be sure that Bergeron will still be a big part of the team as it goes forward. The veteran center will no doubt be vital to leading the Bruins' charge back to the postseason.

CAREER HIGHLIGHTS

Drafted 45th overall by the Boston Bruins in 2003

Member of the Stanley Cup–winning Boston Bruins in 2011

Three-time winner of the Frank J. Selke Trophy (2012, 2014 and 2015)

Winner of the King Clancy Memorial Trophy in 2013

Recorded 206 goals and 550 points in 740 career games

Eastern Conference Team Star

Zemgus GIRGENSONS CENTER 28

Buffalo, however, has been a difficult place to play in the last few seasons, but that may be changing. By finishing in the league basement in 2014–15, the Sabres secured themselves the second-overall selection in the 2015 entry draft. They chose American sensation Jack Eichel, and along with a couple of crafty draft-day trades, the Sabres acquired some high-quality offensive players without having to give up too much. Plus, with the addition of sniper Evander Kane at the trade deadline last season, Buffalo, all of a sudden, is looking like a great city to play in for the 2015–16 campaign. The team will be young and loaded at center, and the enthusiastic energy will be a breath of fresh air for a franchise that has been faltering for years.

Girgensons began his professional career with the Rochester Americans of the American Hockey League (AHL) during the 2012–13 season but got off to a slow start, finishing with just 17 points in 61 games. It was a year marred with injury for Girgensons (he suffered a concussion), but he came back strong in the playoffs by scoring three goals in three postseason games. The Americans were swept by the Toronto Marlies, but Girgensons was one of the best players on his team in the short series, and he scored a highlight-reel goal in the final game. It was in these quarterfinals that he showed how he could handle penalty-killing duties, as well as an aggressive never-say-die approach to the game with his hard-hitting reputation.

Girgensons took this confidence with him to Buffalo for the 2013–14 season and played in 70 games as a rookie, registering 22 points. He was also the only NHL player on the Latvian team that competed at the 2014 Winter Olympics, and he did his country proud with two points in five games played.

The 2014–15 campaign once again saw an injury shorten his year, this time to 61 games, but Girgensons scored 15 times (up from eight the previous year) and totaled 30 points. The people of Latvia made it a point

Buffalo Sabres center Zemgus Girgensons already has one major distinction about him after playing in only two NHL seasons. In fact, this notoriety comes from before he even started playing for the Sabres, as their decision to draft him 14th overall in 2012 made him the highest NHL-drafted player in history from the small country of Latvia. He surpassed the mark once held by retired defenseman Sandis Ozolinsh, who was selected 30th overall by the San Jose Sharks in 1991 and who was a one-time Stanley Cup champion with the Colorado Avalanche in 1996. The 6-foot-1, 190-pound Girgensons hopes to have an even better career than fellow countryman Ozolinsh, and if Girgensons' first two years are any indication, he is off to a good start.

to get their hero into the NHL All-Star Game, and with the help of online voting, Girgensons received the most votes of any player. He didn't score a point in the free-wheeling 17–12 All-Star contest, but he did see over 13 minutes of game action. For a player who arguably didn't deserve to be in the game on skill alone, it was the experience of a lifetime. For Girgensons, the task will be to earn his way back to the game — and that is something Buffalonians might then get on the bandwagon for.

For Girgensons going forward, the question is where on the depth chart he will land. With Eichel and the newly signed Ryan O'Reilly (who had 55 points with the Colorado Avalanche in 2014–15) also on the team, Girgensons will clearly have to fight for ice time at the center position. He may even have to switch to the wing to find more playing time, but the eager 21-year-old looks like he is a force to be reckoned with — and with the backing of an entire nation, he has all the support he needs to succeed.

CAREER HIGHLIGHTS

Drafted 14th overall by the Buffalo Sabres in 2012

Finished second with the Sabres in 2014–15 in shooting percentage, with 13

Elected to the 2015 NHL All-Star Game by fan voting

Recorded 23 goals and 52 points in 131 career games

Eastern Conference Team Star

Eric STAAL

CENTER 12

The fact of the matter is that Staal enjoys playing for the Hurricanes, especially since the organization worked hard to get his brother Jordan onto the team in 2012. And while neither the player nor the team have been faring well in recent years, it is hard to imagine either party requesting a separation.

The 2014–15 campaign was Staal's least productive full season since he was a rookie in 2003. He was hoping for a fresh start, but off-season surgery to repair a torn abdominal muscle derailed that notion. The Hurricanes had also brought in new coach Bill Peters, but neither Eric nor Jordan (who broke his leg in the preseason) could help the new bench boss get off to a good start with the season. The brothers are aware that they are key components in the makeup of the team and each knows how to go all the way since both have Stanley Cup rings (Jordan earned his with the Pittsburgh Penguins in 2009). But when talented players are somewhat alone on a mediocre team, it is difficult for anyone to achieve success.

A big problem for the Hurricanes is that a lot of players on the team haven't performed anywhere near what was expected of them. Goalie Cam Ward has become a shadow of what he once was and left-winger Jeff Skinner has never exceeded what he accomplished as a rookie. The blue line is especially weak with the loss of veteran Joni Pitkanen to injury, but there is hope that Justin Faulk will continue to rise after an amazing 49-point season as a 22-year-old defenseman. Up front, the Hurricanes saw production from 20-year-old Elias Lindholm (39 points) and 21-year-old Victor Rask (33 points), but it wasn't enough and the team finished last in the Metropolitan Division. They did, however, hold the fifth spot in the 2015 entry draft and selected top-rated defenseman Noah Hanifin, who is not only a superstar on the blue line, but also has great scoring capabilities.

Ever the company man, Staal has repeatedly stated that he would do whatever the organization asks of him,

There is no doubt that Eric Staal is a star hockey player. He is a member of the Triple Gold Club, having won the Stanley Cup in 2006, the World Championships in 2007 and an Olympic gold medal in 2010. He has also been playing in the NHL for over 10 years and is the all-time franchise leader for the Carolina Hurricanes in shots, shorthanded goals and hat tricks. And, even though he hasn't won either award, his name comes to mind when thinking of the Lady Byng Memorial Trophy and Frank J. Selke Trophy (he has appeared on both ballots a combined total of nine times). In light of this stellar career, the question to be asked is: why is Staal still playing in Carolina, a team that hasn't made the playoffs in six seasons or finished with over 100 points since their 2006 Stanley Cup win?

even if that means being traded. That scenario doesn't appear too likely, though, as general manager Ron Francis has shown he is in no rush to ship either of the Staals out of Carolina. However, if a team shows enough interest in Staal, which many already have, the return for a player like him would probably be too much for Francis to resist.

The 6-foot-4, 205-pound Staal is still a highly effective athlete. He has played in six full NHL seasons, is 13th on the all-time list for shots on goal for active players and has 47 game-winning goals over his career on a team that tends to lose more than it wins. He is a smart player, and while he's not overly physical, he can be an imposing figure when he wants to show the old-time magic. At 30 years old, Staal still has plenty of gas in the tank, so hopefully his team can match his drive for success in the upcoming seasons.

CAREER HIGHLIGHTS

Drafted 2nd overall by the Carolina Hurricanes in 2003

Member of Stanley Cup–winning Hurricanes team in 2006

Member of Canada's gold-medal team in 2010

Recorded 312 goals and 742 points in 846 career games

Eastern Conference Team Star

Ryan
JOHANSEN

CENTER
19

The Columbus Blue Jackets hosted the NHL All-Star Game for the first time in franchise history in 2015, and it could not have gone any better with their local star being named the Most Valuable Player of the game.

There were plenty of candidates to win the award in a game that ended 17–12 for the team captained by Blue Jackets mainstay Nick Foligno, but it was center Ryan Johansen, his Columbus teammate, who was given the award and the keys to a new car for his two-goal and two-assist performance in front of the hometown crowd.

It was a fitting end to a great weekend for Johansen, who wore an Ohio State Buckeyes sweater for the Skills Competition the day before the game, pleasing the locals with a few stellar moves and funny gags.

Truthfully, it was a bit of a surprise that Johansen was even at the All-Star Game. He had missed training camp due to prolonged contract negotiations with the Blue Jackets and some thought the late start might hurt his season. When all was finally settled, Johansen had a new three-year deal valued at $12 million, which ended up being money well spent. He had 43 points by the All-Star break in late January and finished the season second in team scoring with 71 points, including a team-high 45 assists. He also played in all 82 games, scoring seven power-play goals to go along with two short-handed tallies.

Born in Vancouver, British Columbia, Johansen first came into prominence as a 15-year-old when he recorded 48 points in 41 minor hockey games. He joined the Portland Winterhawks of the WHL as a 17-year-old for the 2009–10 season and caught the eye of NHL scouts with his breakout campaign of 69 points in 71 games. Columbus was happy to snag Johansen with the fourth-overall pick at the 2010 entry draft, but sent him back to the juniors for another season in Portland, where he took the team to the Western Hockey League (WHL) final. He led all playoff scorers with 28 points, but his efforts weren't enough to get past the Kootenay Ice.

The rangy 6-foot-3, 223-pound Johansen jumped into the big league in 2011–12, but he didn't become a full-time NHLer until the 2013–14 season. That breakthrough campaign saw Johansen score 33 goals and 30 assists in 82 games for the Blue Jackets. He added six points in six playoff games, but Columbus lost to the Pittsburgh Penguins in the first round.

Johansen followed up 2013–14 with a stellar 2014–15 season, leading all forwards with a 19:30 average time on ice. The 23-year-old is now considered not only one of the best young players in the NHL but also one of the elite centers in all of hockey. The 2015 All-Star Game nod should be the first of many invites he recieves to the mid-season contest.

Johansen's game is all about being consistently strong on the puck. His size allows him to command attention in front of the net or during the cycle game. And, as all great centermen should be, Johansen is an excellent playmaker with tremendous vision that allows him to make creative passes. Having twice broken the 25-goal mark, opposing goalies also know he can shoot. Much like Ryan Getzlaf, Johansen plays a disciplined game for a big man. He rarely takes penalties, and if he can improve on his defensive game, he will surely be a Frank J. Selke Trophy contender in the years to come.

Columbus' veteran Foligno has taken Johansen under his wing and he pushes the youthful center to strive for more. The playfulness between the two of them was apparent to all who watched the All-Star Game, and as the new captain of the club, Foligno will be encouraging the franchise star even more.

The 2014–15 season was a terrible one for injuries in Columbus, but they are a young team on the rise and if Johansen can keep pace, they should make it back to the postseason soon.

CAREER HIGHLIGHTS

Drafted 4th overall by the Columbus Blue Jackets in 2010

Named 2015 All-Star Game MVP

Tied for first in Columbus for power-play points in 2014–15, with 26

Recorded 73 goals and 167 points in 271 career games

Eastern Conference Team Star

Henrik **ZETTERBERG** LEFT WING **40**

Detroit for the Toronto Maple Leafs, the question is: how will Zetterberg and the other veterans fit into the future plans of the Red Wings and their new coach, Jeff Blashill?

There should be no mistake that Zetterberg can still play hockey. The 34-year-old played in 77 games during the 2014–15 regular season and led his team in points with 66 (even though he scored just 17 times). His team earned 100 points and 43 wins to finish third in the Atlantic Division for its 24th consecutive playoff berth. And while Zetterberg has not scored more than 20 goals or 69 points since 2011–12, he is still a force every time he is out on the ice, as evidenced by his playmaking skills, recording 49 assists in 2014–15 for seventh place in the league. Zetterberg's durability was questioned after back surgery curtailed his 2013–14 season to just 45 games, but he bounced back and ended up with 48 points.

Zetterberg's value is not merely reliant on his point production, but also on his ability to lead his team. He was named captain in 2013 after fellow Swede and legendary defenseman Nicklas Lidstrom retired, and has so far been a fantastic example to his fellow Red Wings. Zetterberg is not selfish with the puck, always having more assists than goals, and he is a skilled clutch player with 59 game-winning goals (good for fourth place in franchise history).

The 6-foot, 190-pound native of Njurunda, Sweden, had an interesting start to his career as a Red Wing. He was chosen in the seventh round of the 1999 entry draft as a player the scouts felt would make a great third-line performer. Soon enough, the Detroit club saw a top two-way player who could produce good numbers on a consistent basis. Zetterberg stayed in Sweden until he was 22 years old, joining the Red Wings roster for the 2002–03 campaign. He nearly won the Calder Memorial Trophy for best rookie with 44 points in 79 games, but lost to St. Louis defenseman Barret Jackman by less than 45 votes. Zetterberg's best year

Perhaps it was inevitable, but any long-time hockey observer is likely still shocked to hear that Henrik Zetterberg's playoff record for the 2015 postseason shows zero goals scored. Since winning the Stanley Cup in 2008 and making it to the final in 2009 (losing the seventh game at home to the Pittsburgh Penguins), the Red Wings have not advanced past the second round and have only managed to win just one of their last five playoff series. Former coach Mike Babcock addressed the issue after the Tampa Bay Lightning ousted the Red Wings in seven games in the 2015 playoffs, stating that his best players (namely, Pavel Datsyuk, Niklas Kronwall and Zetterberg) are long in the tooth and that the younger players on the team, although talented, are not yet ready to win. But now that Babcock has left came in 2007–08 when he recorded 92 points in 75 regular-season games and 27 points in 22 postseason games, helping the Detroit club to win the Stanley Cup for the second time that decade. Zetterberg was awarded the prestigious Conn Smythe Trophy as the playoffs MVP and finished in third for the Frank J. Selke Trophy, which honors the best defensive forward.

Zetterberg was not the only productive veteran who had a great 2014–15 season. Datsyuk had 65 points in 63 games and Kronwall was still racking up opposing players with devastating bodychecks while chipping in 44 points in 80 games. These numbers indicate that the decline of these experienced performers is exaggerated and that they still wear the winged wheel with distinction. Zetterberg is likely to finish his illustrious career in the Motor City, and he will surely continue to add to his already impressive statistics, proving that even late-round draft picks can etch their names in the history books.

CAREER HIGHLIGHTS

Drafted 210th overall by the Detroit Red Wings in 1999

Named captain of the Red Wings in 2013

Winner of the Conn Smythe Trophy in 2008

Olympic gold-medal winner in 2006 with Sweden

Recorded 296 goals and 786 points in 836 career games

Eastern Conference Team Star

Roberto **LUONGO** GOALTENDER 1

and even though he lost 4–2, the spectacle game signified Tortorella's move to make Lack the No. 1 goalie in Vancouver. It was then that Luongo insisted on getting out, and just two days later, the 6-foot-3 netminder was back in Florida playing for the Panthers, a team he had once starred on for five years before going to Vancouver.

Luongo owns a variety of Canucks records, including most career wins (252), most career shutouts (38) and most shutouts in one season (9). He was the last Canuck goalie to take the team all the way to the Stanley Cup final, which he did in 2011, losing to the Boston Bruins in Game 7 at home. He is also one of only a handful of goalies in the history of the NHL — and the only goalie in modern times — to be named team captain.

At first Luongo struggled to get the respect he deserved as a Canuck, having led the league in losses in 2005–06 and 2007–08, but he more than made up for it during the 2010 Olympic Winter Games when he backstopped the host Canadian team to the gold medal. It was a star-studded roster, but there was still enormous pressure to win it all since the Games were held in Vancouver that year. Luongo won all five of his starts and allowed only nine goals as Canada beat the United States on Sidney Crosby's overtime winner. It was a satisfying moment for Luongo as he proved to his detractors that he could win under pressure — even if it wasn't in the NHL.

Florida represented a fresh start for Luongo. With less media scrutiny and a team in the middle of a rebuild, the veteran keeper was able to focus on his game and avoid the constant throng of media posing questions about crease controversies. Heading into the 2014–15 season, the young Panthers squad wasn't expected to do much, but with Luongo shoring up the previously porous Florida net, he went 28–19–12 with a .921 save percentage. He also kept his team in playoff contention for almost the entire season.

Luongo further established his reputation as a battler

On March 2, 2014, netminder Roberto Luongo had reached his limit. Denied the starting assignment for the Vancouver Canucks' outdoor game at BC Place against the Ottawa Senators, Luongo decided he had to press the team for a trade. When the Vancouver club dealt away promising backup Cory Schneider in 2013, it had looked like Luongo was going to stay a Canuck for the rest of his career, especially since he publicly acknowledged that his lucrative contract worked against him in finding a suitable trade partner. But when John Tortorella (known for being rough on goaltenders) took over as coach in 2013, he began to test Luongo's mettle by favoring backup Eddie Lack and pushing Luongo to the bench more and more often. Lack got the start in the outdoor game versus Ottawa,

in the 2014–15 campaign. During a late-season game against the Toronto Maple Leafs, Luongo suffered a shoulder injury and was replaced by backup goaltender Al Montoya. Montoya subsequently tweaked his groin and despite having changed out of his gear, Luongo suited back up to replace his injured teammate. If Luongo hadn't done so, goalie coach Robb Tallas would have had to step in. Luongo's commitment to the team and ability to shrug off an injury for the night was all the talk on sports highlight shows.

Besides his winning attitude, the native of Montreal is good at using his entire 217-pound frame to block a large portion of the net. He is equally adept at covering the bottom of the net with his long legs and quick butterfly as he is fighting back at challenging shooters on his feet. His rebound control is excellent and he is difficult to beat on breakaways because of his length.

With a young and talented Panthers lineup, the cagey veteran between the pipes will be setting the pulse for the team and hopefully helping the Panthers return to the playoffs.

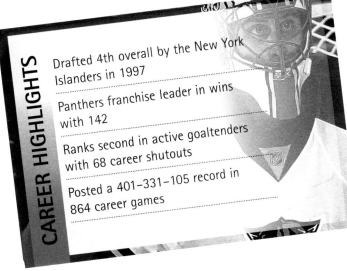

CAREER HIGHLIGHTS

Drafted 4th overall by the New York Islanders in 1997

Panthers franchise leader in wins with 142

Ranks second in active goaltenders with 68 career shutouts

Posted a 401–331–105 record in 864 career games

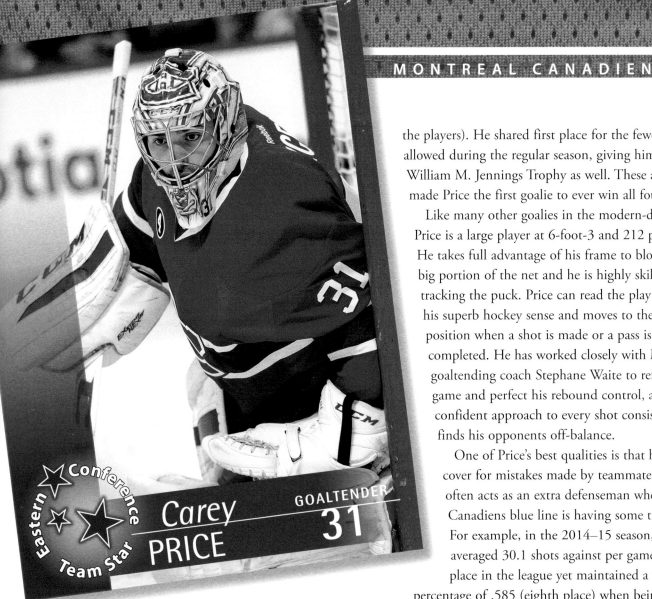

Eastern Conference Team Star

GOALTENDER
Carey
PRICE
31

the players). He shared first place for the fewest goals allowed during the regular season, giving him the William M. Jennings Trophy as well. These awards made Price the first goalie to ever win all four.

Like many other goalies in the modern-day NHL, Price is a large player at 6-foot-3 and 212 pounds. He takes full advantage of his frame to block a big portion of the net and he is highly skilled at tracking the puck. Price can read the play with his superb hockey sense and moves to the correct position when a shot is made or a pass is completed. He has worked closely with Montreal goaltending coach Stephane Waite to refine his game and perfect his rebound control, and this confident approach to every shot consistently finds his opponents off-balance.

One of Price's best qualities is that he can cover for mistakes made by teammates. He often acts as an extra defenseman when the Canadiens blue line is having some trouble. For example, in the 2014–15 season, Montreal averaged 30.1 shots against per game for 21st place in the league yet maintained a winning percentage of .585 (eighth place) when being out-shot. This proves that Montreal's offense-first style of game under coach Michel Therrien works well for this team considering they have such a stellar goaltender in net. Price is also renowned for his cool, calm game; he rarely gets flustered and takes in stride the runs by opponents who crash his crease. His demeanor, how-ever, shouldn't be read as nonchalant because Price is extremely competitive and committed to winning. His composure is inspiring and allows the team to believe they have a chance at winning any game. For Price, this is the perfect mindset to have when playing in a hockey-mad city like Montreal.

Price was taken fifth overall in 2005 as a highly regarded junior performer. He had played for the Tri-City Americans of the Western Hockey League (WHL), where he won 83 games in 193 appearances. He was assigned to the American Hockey League's (AHL's)

Montreal Canadiens goaltender Carey Price had a season for the ages during the NHL's 2014–15 regular campaign. He led the league in save percentage (.933), goals-against average (1.96) and wins (44), the latter setting a franchise record for the most wins in one season. His nine shutouts tied him for second with the Washington Capitals' Braden Holtby, which was just one behind Marc-Andre Fleury of the Pittsburgh Penguins. Price's consistency as goal-tender was the main reason the Habs finished second overall in the Eastern Conference — as well as the entire league — with 110 points (the team's best since 1988–89). Price's outstanding year was recognized with the Hart Trophy (MVP), the Vezina Trophy (best goal-tender) and the Ted Lindsay Award (MVP as voted by

Hamilton Bulldogs in 2006–07 and promptly won the Calder Cup with a great performance in the postseason, winning 15 games with a .936 save percentage. He was promoted to the Canadiens the following season and pegged as the goalie of the future, but in the 2010 playoffs, goaltender Jaroslav Halak stole the spotlight and advanced the Habs to the third round of the playoffs. Naturally, there were those who thought Price would be trade bait but the Canadiens wisely traded Halak and kept Price.

Since he took over in 2010–11 as the number one netminder, Price has come in the top 10 for wins four out of five seasons and sits in fifth on the all-time players list for save percentage (.919). The Canadiens have a long history of great goaltenders — including Hall of Famers Georges Vezina, George Hainsworth, Bill Durnan, Jacques Plante, Gump Worsley, Ken Dryden and Patrick Roy — and it appears Price will

CAREER HIGHLIGHTS

Drafted 5th overall by the Montreal Canadiens in 2005

Recorded 34 career shutouts

Nominated five times for the Vezina Trophy

Set a Canadiens record with 44 wins in 2014–15

Posted a 223-153-50 record in 435 career games

join this group if he can keep playing at his current high standard.

In the immediate future, Montreal has to find some offensive attack in order to support Price, who is the best goalie in the NHL and is very much in his prime at the age of 28. And while Price has won a gold medal with Team Canada at the 2014 Winter Olympics, he now needs a Stanley Cup to put him among the all-time great NHL goaltenders.

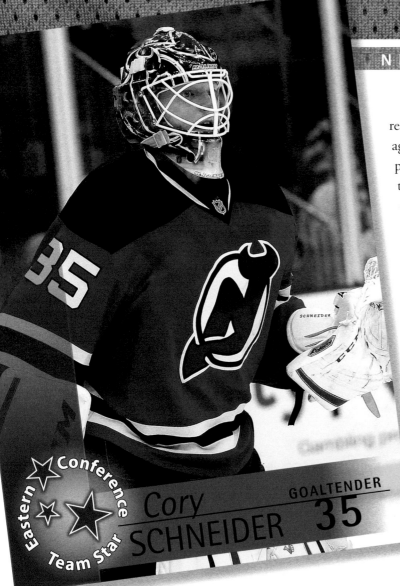

Eastern Conference Team Star

Cory SCHNEIDER

GOALTENDER 35

respectable record of 16–15–12 with a 1.97 goals-against average (which was third-best in the league) playing behind a team that had a lot of offensive trouble. Schneider's performance was enough to convince the Devils not to re-sign Brodeur, so he became a free agent while Schneider took over for the 2014–15 season.

Before becoming a number one goalie in the NHL, Schneider played high school hockey in his home state. He then joined the USA Hockey National Development Program, and in 2003 led Team USA to their first-ever gold medal in the U-18 Junior World Cup. Afterward, he attended Boston College, as his parents insisted he get an education in case of a career-ending injury. Schneider wound up leaving school early, but still managed to get his degree in finance over three summers of study. During his time as a Boston College Eagle, Schneider won 66 games in 99 appearances, posted a 2.09 goals-against average and earned all-star honors in 2005 and 2006. Not quite ready for the NHL, Schneider was assigned to the Manitoba Moose of the American Hockey League (AHL). He posted an 84–45–5 record and anyone who saw him play knew he was destined for the big league. Schneider was especially good at winning close games and his goals-against average while playing for the Moose never rose above 2.51. In 2008–09, he took the Manitoba team to the Calder Cup final for the first time before losing to the Hershey Bears. Schneider won the award for the goalie on the team with the fewest goals-against, as well as the Goaltender of the Year award.

After advancing to the NHL, Schneider's time in Vancouver was well spent, even if it was primarily in a backup role. As a Canuck, he posted an impressive 86–55–26 record and tied for first in shutouts in 2012–13. He also shared the William M. Jennings Trophy (awarded to the goalie or goalies with the fewest goals scored against in a minimum of 25 games played during the regular season) with his goaltending

It was the opportunity Marblehead, Massachusetts, native Cory Schneider had been waiting for since he was drafted into the NHL in 2004 — the chance to become a starting goaltender — and it looked like it might happen with the Vancouver Canucks after five years of serving as apprentice to Roberto Luongo. But, when the Canucks couldn't move Luongo's hefty contract, they decided instead to try and get a good return on what many fans perceived to be a number one goalie. Enter the New Jersey Devils. They offered their number one selection in the 2013 entry draft in exchange for Schneider. The trouble was the Devils still had the legendary Martin Brodeur on their roster. Schneider ended up splitting the netminding duties with Brodeur for the 2013–14 season and posted a colleague Luongo in 2010–11. While in New Jersey, his 2014–15 season consisted of 26 wins in 69 appearances playing behind one of the worst offensive teams in the NHL (the Devils scored only 181 goals in a year when the league average was 224). Of his 69 games played, he stood in net for 31 during which he faced 30-plus shots, and managed to win 14 of them. The workload didn't seem to bother the 6-foot-2, 200-pound goalie, who seemed to thrive once he became accustomed to being in the crease almost every night. To top it off, Schneider ended up

posting an amazing .925 save percentage, good for fifth in the league.

Schneider is a positional goalie who uses his size strategically, rarely flops on the ice and makes almost every save seem like a routine stop. His ability to anticipate plays will help him in the NHL for years to come, especially since he is only 29 years old. Schneider's contract takes him to the end of the 2021–22 season, so it is every fan's hope that the Devils will acquire more offensive and defensive talent in order to help him out.

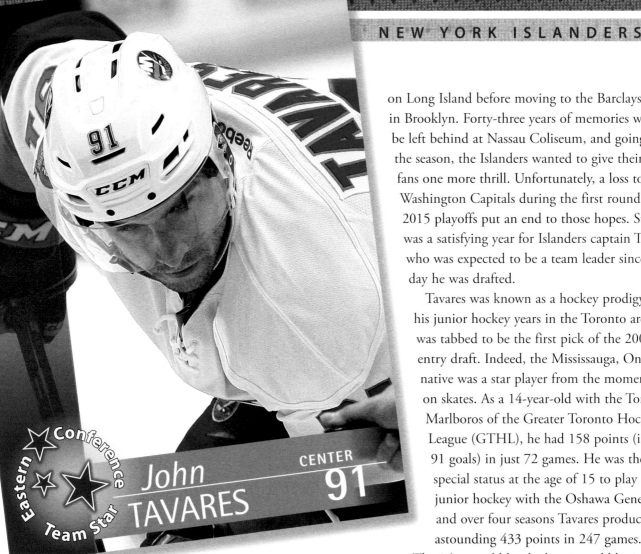

Eastern Conference Team Star

John
TAVARES

CENTER
91

on Long Island before moving to the Barclays Center in Brooklyn. Forty-three years of memories were to be left behind at Nassau Coliseum, and going into the season, the Islanders wanted to give their loyal fans one more thrill. Unfortunately, a loss to the Washington Capitals during the first round of the 2015 playoffs put an end to those hopes. Still, it was a satisfying year for Islanders captain Tavares, who was expected to be a team leader since the day he was drafted.

Tavares was known as a hockey prodigy during his junior hockey years in the Toronto area and was tabbed to be the first pick of the 2009 NHL entry draft. Indeed, the Mississauga, Ontario, native was a star player from the moment he put on skates. As a 14-year-old with the Toronto Marlboros of the Greater Toronto Hockey League (GTHL), he had 158 points (including 91 goals) in just 72 games. He was then given special status at the age of 15 to play major junior hockey with the Oshawa Generals, and over four seasons Tavares produced an astounding 433 points in 247 games.

The 24-year-old has had an incredible six-season career with the Islanders, a team that has not been quite as successful as in its Stanley Cup years of the 1980s. The Islanders saw Tavares as a savior for an organization that hasn't won a playoff series since 1993. Tavares was productive right from the start, recording 54 points in his first year (a points total that gave him second place among rookies in the 2009–10 season). His second year saw him record 67 points and his third year was even better with 81 points in 82 games. But, despite Tavares' personal success, the Islanders still floundered. They managed to snag a playoff spot during the lockout-shortened season, but suffered a quick first-round exit against the Pittsburgh Penguins. Fans started to wonder if Tavares had what it takes to lead a team to glory, but nobody was more determined to succeed than the 6-foot-1, 209-pound athlete.

Upon entering the NHL, Tavares' seemingly only flaw

The New York Islanders' star center John Tavares almost had a dream season during the 2014–15 campaign. After suffering a serious knee injury while competing for Canada at the 2014 Winter Olympics, it was unclear if Tavares would be back for the following season, but he ended up playing the complete 82-game schedule and almost won the NHL scoring race with 86 points (he was edged out on the last day of the season by Jamie Benn of the Dallas Stars, who wound up with 87). Tavares' elevated play landed him in eighth place on the Islanders' all-time list of goals per game and he led the team to the playoffs for the second time in three years.

The 2014–15 season was an important one for the New York–based team, which was playing its last year

was his skating speed, but he took the time to develop that part of his game and is now a completely different skater. The Islanders' assistant coach Doug Weight also helped Tavares change his leadership approach, turning him into a role model on and off the ice. Tavares is not only considered the Isles' most important player, he is also an NHL leader among the likes of Sidney Crosby and Jonathan Toews.

In the opening round of the 2015 playoffs, Tavares nearly pushed the Islanders past the Capitals when he scored his first-ever postseason overtime goal for a win on home ice. That goal gave the New York club a 2–1 lead in the series, but Washington came back to edge out the Islanders in seven games. It appears, however, that the Islanders have turned a corner with better defense and goaltending (Jaroslav Halak created a franchise record of 38 wins in 2014–15), as well as with additional

forwards who can help Tavares provide more offense.

The fans on Long Island will not see another title on their home turf, but those who follow the team to Brooklyn might get to feel the pride of a banner hanging from the rafters of a new arena — Tavares and the Islanders just need to keep improving.

CAREER HIGHLIGHTS

Drafted 1st overall by the New York Islanders in 2009

Named team captain in 2013

Finished twice in the league's top 5 for goals scored (2012–13 and 2014–15)

Named to the NHL's First All-Star Team in 2015

Recorded 174 goals and 401 points in 432 career games

Eastern Conference Team Star

Rick
NASH

LEFT WING
61

end to it all in front of the Los Angeles crowd.

In a way, the play that Nash couldn't complete was typical of how the entire 2014 postseason went for the scoring star of the Rangers — no luck and little production. In 25 playoff games Nash had only three goals and 10 points, which was well below expectations for the 6-foot-4, 192-pound native of Brampton, Ontario, who was the first-overall selection of the 2002 NHL entry draft.

In fairness to Nash, he only played in 65 games in 2013–14 (scoring 26 goals) because he suffered a severe concussion during the third game of the regular season. He started the 2014–15 season determined to do much better. Nash dedicated himself to a strong off-season conditioning program that brought him to the Rangers training camp in top form. His stellar condition didn't go unnoticed after he scored a career-high 42 goals during the regular season, took 304 shots on goal (second only to Alex Ovechkin of Washington) and led the league with 32 even-strength goals, making him a feared offensive force once more.

Unfortunately, once the 2015 playoffs began, Nash's numbers were not enough to help the Rangers to the final again. He was better than the year before, putting up 14 points in 19 games, and tied for first in the most postseason shots on goal with 69. He was excellent defensively (finishing with a plus-8 rating) and played an all-around team game, but he only scored five times. The Rangers simply needed more from their star.

Nash came to the Rangers in a deal with the Columbus Blue Jackets after he and the team concluded it would be better for all concerned if he was moved (he did a lot for the franchise, but couldn't translate that into team success). New York paid a heavy price for the former junior star of the London Knights — they gave up three young players and a first-round draft choice. In return, they wanted results from Nash, who had led the NHL in goals in just his second year (41 in 2003–04) and who had clicked for 289 career goals while with Columbus.

R ick Nash of the New York Rangers had a terrible playoff season in 2014, even though his team made it to the Stanley Cup final for the first time since 1994 (when they last won the Cup). In the final, the Rangers faced off against the Los Angeles Kings, but the latter team proved to be too strong and took the Rangers out in five games.

During the fifth and last contest, Nash had a great opportunity to score the winning goal against Kings goalie Jonathan Quick, who appeared to be at his mercy. Nash's shot, however, was deflected by a defenseman's stick and the Rangers' best chance to win the game was gone. If Nash had scored, the sixth game of the series would have been back in New York, but shortly after Nash's attempt, Kings blue-liner Alec Martinez put an

Nash has the size to be termed a power forward, but he is not overly aggressive and has the finesse of a much smaller player. When he is at his best, he can score with his superior shot from virtually anywhere on the ice and he can be used in all types of playmaking situations, including the power play and penalty kill. This well-rounded style is a big reason why he was chosen to play for Team Canada at two Olympic Winter Games, which allowed him to win a pair of gold medals.

Despite two disappointing postseasons, the 31-year-old Nash has had an incredible career so far and has improved immensely over his 12 seasons in the NHL (he went from minus-71 in Columbus to plus-55 in New York). He has helped the Rangers improve their regular season numbers since arriving in New York, but Nash has to find a way to excel in the playoffs or else he might be on the move again depending on how new general manager Jeff Gorton views his star players.

CAREER HIGHLIGHTS

Drafted 1st overall by the Columbus Blue Jackets in 2002

Shared winner of Maurice Richard Trophy in 2003–04

Ranks sixth in Rangers history for goals per game

Has scored 30-plus goals in a season eight times

Recorded 378 goals and 697 points in 862 career games

Eastern Conference
Team Star

Erik
KARLSSON

DEFENSE
65

goaltender Andrew Hammond was brought in to start and the Senators suddenly became unstoppable. They went 21–3–3 from that point until the end of the regular season and officially clinched a playoff spot with 99 points. The Montreal Canadiens knocked Ottawa out in the first round, but not before the Senators gave the Habs a tough six-game battle.

One of the biggest reasons for the Senators' remarkable turnaround was the great play put out by Karlsson, one of the team's most talented players. Under MacLean, the Swedish Karlsson was not playing his best hockey, but when Cameron took over, he gave Karlsson more ice time and the green light to lead offensive attacks. By the end of the season, Karlsson was averaging close to 30 minutes per game and had boosted his offensive production to 66 points (the best of all blue-liners in the league), which earned him the 2015 James Norris Memorial Trophy for best defenseman. He now sits in the franchise record books in sixth for assists, fourth in assists per game and tenth in goals created.

He had finally returned to the form that had once made him the best defenseman in the league.

Karlsson was originally selected 15th overall by the Senators in 2008 and was the seventh defenseman chosen in the first round of that draft. It is interesting to note that none of the blue-liners selected ahead of Karlsson have won the Norris Trophy, which he did for the first time in 2012 when he recorded 78 points in 81 games. His point total put him in the top 10 for all scorers that season while no other blue-liner even made the top 20.

Karlsson's superior skill set is built around his skating and speed. He can turn on the jets to lead the attack or hurry back to cover his own end. His stretch passes can catch the opposition off guard and his work on the Senators' power play is superb. Karlsson's control of the point with the extra man tends to give the Ottawa side a huge advantage and he led his team with 30 power-play points in 2014–15. The Senators also finished in 11th

When the Ottawa Senators dismissed head coach Paul MacLean early in the 2014–15 season, there was a sense of relief throughout the organization. It's not that MacLean was a bad coach (his final record in Ottawa was 114–90–35 and he won the Jack Adams Award in 2013), but it was evident that he wasn't getting the best out of some of the younger players on the squad. One player in particular who seemed to be floundering was team captain Erik Karlsson. After MacLean was fired, assistant coach Dave Cameron took over his position and was left to deal with a deflated team that had posted an 11–11–5 record for the season thus far. For a while it seemed as if the team was going to continue at this pace, but things finally changed in mid-February 2015. Backup

place for penalty killing, which was a jump from 21st the season before — Karlsson undeniably having a big part in that growth. Since he is not a large player, the 6-foot, 175-pound Karlsson tends to not involve himself in the more physical side of the game, but he is also not averse to hitting the opposition when necessary in order to make a play. Karlsson has adjusted well to being the captain of the Senators and to the responsibility that comes with the position. It could be said that the 25-year-old enjoys the attention his role as captain brings, as he likes to wear his hair long and is considered one of the more fashionable players in the league.

The Senators have inserted many younger players into their lineup (such as Cody Ceci, Mike Hoffman, Curtis Lazar, Mark Stone and Mika Zibanejad), and it is management's hope that they can look to Karlsson's leadership to guide the team to a more consistent play-off position in the years to come.

CAREER HIGHLIGHTS

Drafted 15th overall by the Ottawa Senators in 2008

Winner of the James Norris Memorial Trophy in 2012 and 2015

Named to the NHL's First All-Star Team in 2012 and 2015

Recorded 84 goals and 303 points in 397 career games

Eastern Conference Team Star

Claude **GIROUX**

CENTER **28**

The Philadelphia Flyers' Claude Giroux is the kind of player a team wants to have on its side. Not only is he one of the most skilled athletes in hockey, he is a self-proclaimed trash-talker (which started when he played hockey with his friends as a kid) and enjoys getting under the skin of his opposition. In particular, Pittsburgh Penguin Sidney Crosby has had major disagreements with Giroux, specifically in the 2012 playoffs. The two captains played well together at the 2015 IIHF World Hockey Championships, but when the 2015–16 season gets underway, Giroux will go back to being Crosby's competitor, especially since both of these division rivals are itching for more postseason success.

Giroux's path to NHL stardom was not something

that was foreseen for the native of Hearst, Ontario. On the smallish side, Giroux didn't play major junior hockey until he was 18 years old, but a good season with 40 points in 48 games for the Ontario Junior-A Cumberland Grads earned him a tryout with the Gatineau Olympiques of the Quebec Major Junior Hockey League (QMJHL). The Olympiques' coach was Benoit Groulx and he was quickly impressed by Giroux's wizardry with the puck. Giroux racked up over 100 points in each of his three seasons with the team, including 103 points in his first season. The timing was excellent because Giroux's superb rookie year as an Olympique in 2005–06 coincided with the first time he was eligible for the NHL draft. Groulx had done a masterful job of preparing Giroux for professional hockey, and after two scouts from the Philadelphia Flyers took an interest in his game and competitive nature, Giroux became the first-round draft choice of the Flyers (22nd overall) in 2006.

Giroux was allowed to finish his junior eligibility with the Olympiques and then he briefly played in the American Hockey League (AHL) for the Philadelphia Phantoms (with 36 points in 38 games) before joining the Flyers midway through the 2008–09 season. In his second NHL campaign, Giroux had a respectable 47 points in 82 games, but really proved himself in the 2010 playoffs when the Flyers made it all the way to the Stanley Cup final against the Chicago Blackhawks. He had 21 points in 23 games, including the overtime-winning goal in Game 3 for Philadelphia's first win of the series. His outstanding playoff performance gave him the boost he needed to see himself as a true NHL player and the 2010–11 regular season was a breakout year for the swift-skating Giroux. He led his team in points (76), assists (51), shorthanded goals (3) and was the only forward to play more than an average of 19 minutes a game. He soon became a point-per-game player and achieved a career-best 93 points in 2011–12, good enough for third in NHL scoring that season.

In 2013–14, the 5-foot-11, 172-pound Giroux notched 86 points, earning him another third place in scoring and a Hart Memorial Trophy nomination for NHL MVP. He continued to play well in 2014–15, but slipped back to 73 points (the 10th best mark in the NHL scoring race). His team also missed out on the playoffs for the second time in three years. Overall, however, Giroux has proven himself to be an outstanding playmaker and someone who has great vision on the ice, especially when it comes to the power play (he had a team-leading 37 power-play points in 2014–15, almost half of his 76 point total).

The Flyers named Dave Hakstol out of the University of North Dakota as their new coach for the beginning of the 2015–16 season, and Giroux should thrive under Hakstol, who wants the Philadelphia club to adapt to the more modern style of NHL play. This new mentor also promises to emphasize skill and speed, which should mean plenty of ice time for the confident 27-year-old team captain and number one Flyers center.

CAREER HIGHLIGHTS

Drafted 22nd overall by the Philadelphia Flyers in 2006

Named team captain in 2013

Has finished in the top 10 in NHL assists five times

Recorded 144 goals and 450 points in 496 career games

Nill wisely made the most talented player on the squad the team captain and the Canadians went undefeated throughout the entire tournament. Crosby finished with 4 goals and 11 points in 9 games, including a goal and an assist in the final 6–1 romp over Canada's rival, Russia.

Seeing "Sid the Kid'" with a grin on his face as he lifted the IIHF trophy was a nice contrast to his recent frustrations in the NHL. While his personal numbers are always at or near the top (he finished third in scoring with 84 points in 2014–15), Crosby's team continues to struggle in the play-offs, and another quick exit in the 2014–15 postseason did nothing to boost the Penguins star. Since he joined the NHL in 2005–06 as an 18-year-old, hockey fans have expected Crosby to regularly lead the Penguins to the Stanley Cup final. The reality is that since the Pittsburgh club won the championship in 2009, the Penguins have not moved past the conference finals. Crosby's production in the postseason is still strong with 118 points in 100 career playoff games, but he is no longer dominating the way he once did. The Penguins have been plagued with particularly serious medical issues on their defensive line, including Olli Maatta's tumor removal and Kris Letang's stroke. The goaltending of Marc-Andre Fleury has not been consistent either — he is one of the best regular season netminders, coming in the top 10 for wins since 2008–09, but only managed one postseason victory in 2015.

Because of these issues, Penguins fans may be anticipating changes on the bench, but Crosby, for one, is comfortable playing in Pittsburgh, a city that appreciates superstars but prevents them from being swarmed with too much attention. For example, Hall of Famer Mario Lemieux views Pittsburgh as a first-rate city after spending his entire career there and is currently a co-owner of the franchise.

As for Crosby, he is aware of his status as one of the best players in the NHL but has handled his success

Eastern Conference Team Star

Sidney CROSBY

CENTER 87

In 2015, Sidney Crosby became the 26th member of what is known in hockey circles as the Triple Gold Club. He earned his membership with Team Canada's win at the 2015 IIHF World Championships in Prague, but his venture into the club started in 2009 when he won the Stanley Cup with the Pittsburgh Penguins and then took two Olympic gold medals in 2010 and 2014. Crosby is also the only player among the 26 members to have captained all his winning teams.

There was a chance Crosby may not have been able to play at the Worlds. The tournament began during the NHL playoffs and the Penguins were battling the New York Rangers in the first round, but when the Penguins were knocked out, Crosby made a phone call to Team Canada general manager Jim Nill and said he was in.

maturely. He makes himself accessible to the media and is unlikely to make confrontational comments. He has also made a major contribution to the local community by outfitting thousands of young kids, year after year, with hockey equipment, often providing the funding out of his own pocket.

It is the combination of Crosby's talents, leadership and selfless community service that makes him so well-liked among his colleagues. He has won the Ted Lindsay Award three times, an honor that is handed out to the most outstanding player as selected by the NHL Players Association. He is also the active players leader in goals created per game (0.49), assists per game (0.88) and points per game (1.36), the latter placing him fifth on the all-time list ahead of greats like Guy Lafleur and Joe Sakic.

A four-time First Team All-Star, Crosby has accomplished a lot in his NHL career, but at only 28 years old, Sid the Kid is well positioned to attain plenty more success.

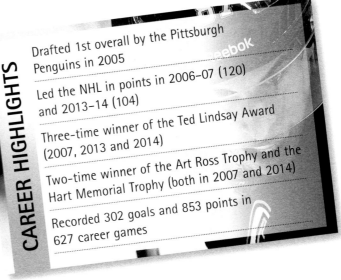

CAREER HIGHLIGHTS

Drafted 1st overall by the Pittsburgh Penguins in 2005

Led the NHL in points in 2006–07 (120) and 2013–14 (104)

Three-time winner of the Ted Lindsay Award (2007, 2013 and 2014)

Two-time winner of the Art Ross Trophy and the Hart Memorial Trophy (both in 2007 and 2014)

Recorded 302 goals and 853 points in 627 career games

Eastern Conference Team Star

Steven STAMKOS

CENTER 91

spending the summer trying to move past the loss in order to come back for the 2015–16 season.

That painful postseason was not the first time Stamkos had to face adversity. When he first arrived in Tampa Bay in 2008, he had to deal with coach Barry Melrose, who suggested that as an 18-year-old, Stamkos wasn't strong enough for the NHL, even though he had been selected first overall by the Lightning. Melrose didn't last long in Tampa Bay, but his point got under Stamkos' skin and the 6-foot, 190-pound center has been a workout fanatic ever since. This dedication has helped him bring energy and leadership to his team-mates, which is why he was named captain when Martin St. Louis left for the New York Rangers in 2014. More hardship came when Stamkos broke his leg in November 2013, which held him back from participating on the eventual gold-medal-winning Team Canada at the 2014 Winter Olympics.

Overall, Stamkos has had some amazing moments since coming into the NHL. In just his second season, the hard-shooting Stamkos scored 51 times to win the 2010 Maurice Richard Trophy for most goals. Two years later he did it again when he notched 60 goals and led in game-winning goals (12) as well as even-strength goals (48). He has been named to the Second All-Star Team twice and has led the Lightning in goals for five out of seven seasons. Additionally, Stamkos has revitalized the Tampa Bay franchise and enjoys playing in a non-traditional hockey market.

Stamkos, a native of Markham, Ontario, is used to success in hockey. He was drafted first overall by the Sarnia Sting in the 2006 Ontario Hockey League (OHL) draft, and over two seasons he recorded 197 points in 124 games, making him the top-ranked prospect available for drafting in 2008. Seven years later, he sits on the Lightning's all-time leaders list in third for points (498), first in shooting percentage (17.2) and first in goals per game (0.56). He also holds several single-

T he 2015 Stanley Cup playoffs were a great learn-ing experience for Tampa Bay Lightning captain Steven Stamkos. The star hockey player dis-covered firsthand how difficult it is to advance in each round while trying to fulfill personal expectations as well as those of everyone else. The 25-year-old struggled in Round 1 against the Detroit Red Wings, recording only three assists in seven games. He regained his confidence in the next two rounds against the Montreal Canadiens and New York Rangers with 14 points in 13 games. However, the prolific goal scorer tapered off in the Stanley Cup final against the Chicago Blackhawks and his team lost in six games. Stamkos had plenty of chances to put the puck in the net, but goalposts and deflections kept him off the score sheet, so he will be season records in Tampa Bay, including the most goals, power-play goals and game-winning goals. Stamkos is the prototypical franchise player and has put the Lightning on the map within a tough division.

Coach Jon Cooper ended up moving Stamkos from center to the wing during the 2015 post-season to try and mix things up, but Stamkos only finished with 18 points and averaged just over 18 minutes a game. To his credit, Stamkos never complained and the team played hard throughout four rounds of playoffs (while also learning from their mistakes for next season).

As captain, Stamkos has a great example to follow in Steve Yzerman, the Lightning's general manger who captained the Detroit Red Wings to three titles by playing well at both ends of the ice. When the 2015

playoffs were over, Yzerman said his top priority was to sign Stamkos to a long-term deal, and this suits Stamkos just fine — he has said he wants to win it all in Tampa Bay. True, the Lightning might have to pay a heavy price to keep him, but it will be worth every penny for one of the best snipers in the NHL.

CAREER HIGHLIGHTS

- Drafted 1st overall by the Tampa Bay Lightning in 2008
- Has 35 points in 48 playoff games
- Two-time winner of the Maurice Richard Trophy
- Recorded 276 goals and 498 points in 492 career games

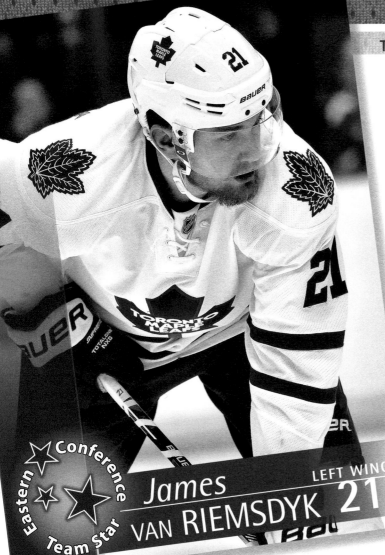

Eastern Conference Team Star

James
VAN RIEMSDYK **LEFT WING 21**

Flyers ended up making it all the way to the Stanley Cup final in 2010 for the first time since 1997, with van Riemsdyk contributing six points in 21 games. Philadelphia eventually lost in six games to the Chicago Blackhawks, but van Riemsdyk followed up the 2010–11 season with 40 points and a plus-15 rating (up from minus-1 the year before). His future looked to be on track in the City of Brotherly Love.

The 2011–12 campaign, however, saw the large winger slump to 11 goals while playing in just 43 games. Suddenly, he was seen as a soft player with little gumption for the way the Philadelphia club traditionally liked to play hockey. The Flyers wanted rugged, physical defensemen and soon found out the Toronto Maple Leafs were willing to move blue-liner Luke Schenn. Toronto, on the other hand, was looking to add a large forward to their small but swift attack. Thus, the one-for-one swap was completed in June 2012. Three years later, the Flyers are still hoping to get more out of Schenn (who is often a healthy scratch), while the Maple Leafs acquired one of their best forwards in the deal.

Because of the shortened 2012–13 season, van Riemsdyk didn't get off to a blazing start in Toronto, but he still managed to end the year with 18 goals and a respectable 32 points scored throughout the entire 48-game schedule. He closed out the year with seven points during the infamous seven-game postseason loss to the Boston Bruins. The next season saw van Riemsdyk record a career-high in several categories, including goals (30), assists (31), points (61), penalty minutes (50), power-play goals (9), shorthanded goals (2) and average time on ice (21:03). His play around the opposition's net was something to behold, as he could consistently stick the puck into the top corners of the net using his enviable hand-eye coordination. He was never overly physical, but the first-line winger used his large frame to great effectiveness by planting himself in front of the net, making it virtually impossible for other players to move him.

When the Philadelphia Flyers selected 6-foot-3, 200-pound winger James van Riemsdyk second overall in 2007, the team strongly believed they had chosen a power forward who would be a franchise player for years to come. Before being drafted, the native of Middletown, New Jersey, honed his skills in the USA Hockey National Team Development Program, helping him to win gold in the 2006 IIHF U-18 Championships. He then attended the University of New Hampshire, where he scored 74 points in 67 games before joining the Flyers to start the 2009–10 campaign. As a 20-year-old rookie, van Riemsdyk recorded 35 points, good for eighth place among rookies that year, and he also tied for first among rookies with six game-winning goals. The

The 2014–15 season was more difficult. After Toronto got off to a good start (they held a wild-card spot for the first half of the season), the team fired head coach Randy Carlyle around Christmastime, which was the beginning of the end. The team wound up out of the playoffs with the fourth-worst record in the league, and a once-promising season saw van Riemsdyk end the year with 56 points when, at one point, it looked like 70 points was within easy reach. The Leafs' big line featuring Phil Kessel, Tyler Bozak and van Riemsdyk fell apart when they couldn't figure out how to play effectively under interim-head-coach Peter Horachek (the three players combined for a minus-101 by the end of the season).

The question now being asked is whether new head coach Mike Babcock will keep van Riemsdyk as a building block for a team in upheaval or will he use him as trade bait to get a package of draft picks and/or players. Either way, the talented van Riemsdyk has a strong future ahead of him as he enters the prime years of his career.

Eastern Conference Team Star

Alex OVECHKIN

LEFT WING 8

2014–15 season. He once again led the NHL in goals scored with 53, which made him the only player in the league to hit the 50-goals-scored mark. He scored his 50th of the season on March 31, 2015, when he beat Carolina Hurricanes goalie Cam Ward in the first period of the game. The goal marked the sixth time Ovechkin has scored at least 50 goals in one season, putting him in rare company with the likes of Hall of Fame greats such as Mike Bossy, Wayne Gretzky, Mario Lemieux, Guy Lafleur and Marcel Dionne (all of whom scored 50 or more goals at least six times in their careers). Ovechkin also managed to improve to a plus-10, which factored into the Captials placing second in their division and making the playoffs. They edged out the New York Islanders in seven games in the first round and had the New York Rangers down 3–1 before losing the final three contests to once again miss out on the Eastern Conference final. Ovechkin, for all his awards and honors, has never made it to the conference championship series, let alone a Stanley Cup final, and this fact remains a black mark on his otherwise stellar record.

The native of Moscow has been a great force in the NHL since he was selected first overall by Washington in the 2004 entry draft. His rookie year saw him score 52 goals and total 106 points, taking the 2006 Calder Trophy as the NHL's best rookie over Sidney Crosby. Two years later, he scored an amazing 65 times and his goal-scoring prowess was the talk of the league. Not surprisingly, he was named the winner of the Hart Memorial Trophy as the NHL's best player. His offensive performance over his 10-year career has been incredibly consistent and he is still one of the most feared snipers in all of hockey.

The Capitals, however, have not been fortunate in the postseason and have gone through a series of coaches as a result. Bruce Boudreau, Dale Hunter and Adam Oates have each tried to get the team to perform better in the regular season and playoffs, but over a combined seven years only ever got mixed results. After missing

For Alex Ovechkin, the last two seasons have been contrasting ones. The 2013–14 season was forgettable for the Washington Capitals left-winger, despite scoring a league-leading 51 goals. Ovechkin was a minus-35, his team missed the playoffs for the first time in seven years and he played poorly in the 2014 Winter Olympics in Sochi, Russia. The 6-foot-3, 231-pound Ovechkin wanted to play well for his home country, but the Russians fell to Finland in the quarterfinals of the tournament. His personal life also took a hit when his father underwent heart surgery just as the Olympic Games were taking place. Putting hockey on the back burner, Ovechkin went to be with his father, who, fortunately, recovered.

Ovechkin recovered as well, just in time for the

the 2014 postseason, the Capitals turned to Barry Trotz to run the bench for the 2014–15 campaign. After spending 15 years with the Nashville Predators, his expereince in building a team from the ground up was exactly what the Capitals needed. Upon getting the job in Washington, Trotz told Ovechkin he needed to continue scoring goals and that his plus/minus total had to improve dramatically. Ovechkin heeded the coach's advice and played a more determined game. The goals piled up and the Capitals were back in the playoffs with 45 wins and 101 points (the team's best total since 2010–11). Capitalizing on this success will help the team move forward in 2015–16 in order to get past the second round of the playoffs.

Ovechkin thrives on using his tremendous strength, which helps create an abundance of scoring opportunities. He is especially good on the power play, where he scored a league-leading 25 goals in 2014–15. His one-time slap-shot is incredibly accurate and his teammates feed him

the puck at every opportunity. Ovechkin is also team captain, a six-time First Team All-Star and a five-time winner of the Maurice "Rocket" Richard Trophy for top goal-scorer (the most anyone has ever won it).

The Capitals have worked hard to improve their team, and their continual progress will surely help Ovechkin to lead them all the way.

CAREER HIGHLIGHTS

Drafted 1st overall by the Washington Capitals in 2004

Three-time winner of both the Hart Trophy and Ted Lindsay Award

Led the NHL five times in goals scored

Named to the NHL's First All-Star Team seven times (2006–2010, 2013, 2015)

Recorded 475 goals and 895 points in 760 career games

WESTERN CONFERENCE TEAM STARS

The best of the Central and Pacific Divisions.

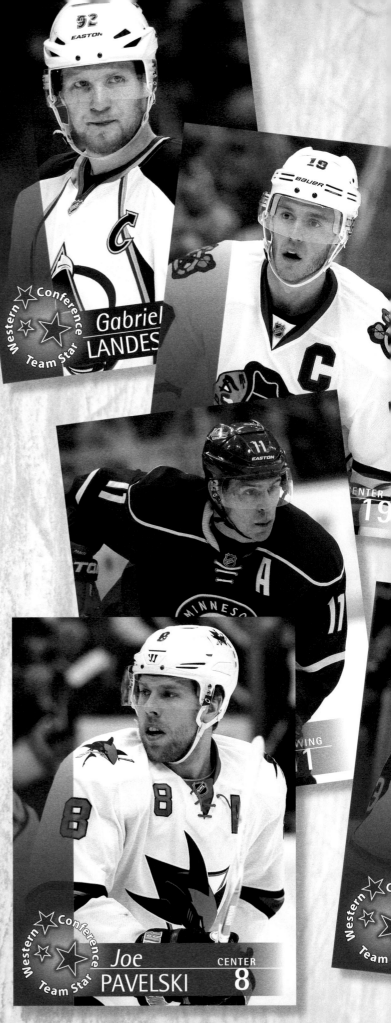

Western Conference Team Star

Gabriel LANDES

Western Conference Team Star

Mark

DEFENSE

Western Conference Team Star

Joe PAVELSKI

CENTER
8

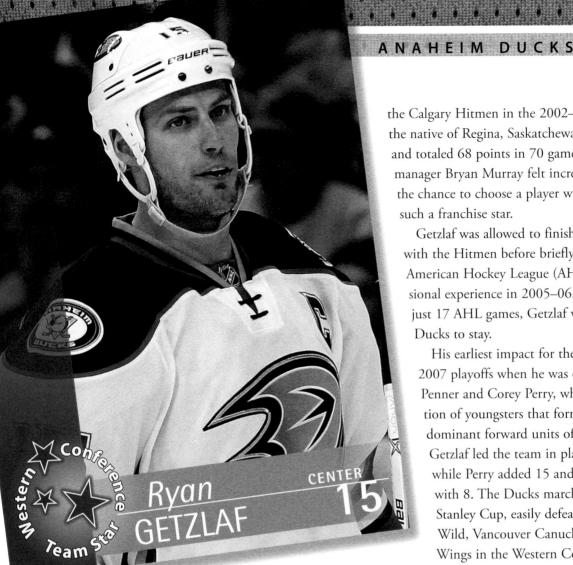

Western Conference Team Star

Ryan GETZLAF

CENTER 15

the Calgary Hitmen in the 2002–03 season when the native of Regina, Saskatchewan, scored 29 goals and totaled 68 points in 70 games. Then-general manager Bryan Murray felt incredibly lucky to have the chance to choose a player who would turn into such a franchise star.

Getzlaf was allowed to finish his junior career with the Hitmen before briefly going to the American Hockey League (AHL) for some professional experience in 2005–06. After 33 points in just 17 AHL games, Getzlaf was brought up to the Ducks to stay.

His earliest impact for the Ducks came in the 2007 playoffs when he was on a line with Dustin Penner and Corey Perry, which was a combination of youngsters that formed one of the most dominant forward units of the postseason. Getzlaf led the team in playoff points with 17, while Perry added 15 and Penner chipped in with 8. The Ducks marched all the way to the Stanley Cup, easily defeating the Minnesota Wild, Vancouver Canucks and Detroit Red Wings in the Western Conference playoffs before running over Ottawa in just five games to win Anaheim's first-ever championship.

The team has been strong ever since, only missing the postseason twice, but it hasn't quite been able to repeat the success of 2007. Still, there can be no complaints about the performance the Ducks get from Getzlaf. He is a consistent producer and is nearly a point-per-game player with 678 in 710 games. He posted a career-high 91 points in 2008–09, has been in the top 10 in the league for assists in 5 out of 10 seasons and has led the Ducks in points for the last three seasons. He was also a key cog in the lineup of two Olympic gold-medal-winning Canadian teams (2010 and 2014). Further, in 2013–14, Getzlaf was nominated to the Second All-Star Team and was second in voting for the NHL's most valuable player, finishing behind Sidney Crosby for the Hart Memorial Trophy.

The 2014–15 season was another good one for

Anaheim Ducks center Ryan Getzlaf is one of the most complete players in the entire NHL. With his big 6-foot-4, 218-pound frame, he is a top playmaker who sees the ice well and often makes it impossible to get the puck off his stick once he has control. He uses his size to his advantage by bumping and grinding the opposition, but is not a reckless sort because he knows he is much more valuable on the ice than in the penalty box. Since being drafted 19th overall by the Ducks in 2003, Getzlaf's role has expanded to the point where he is now the undisputed leader of the team (he was named as captain in 2010), but back in 2003, the Ducks weren't even expecting Getzlaf to be available when it was their turn to select. Anaheim had been impressed with Getzlaf's junior performance with

Getzlaf, who had 45 assists and 70 points. The Ducks helped out their number one center by acquiring Ryan Kesler when they completed a major deal with Vancouver. The new addition meant opposing teams had two top centers to worry about and that helped spread out defensive coverage. The Ducks also won 51 games during the regular season and breezed past the first two rounds of the 2015 postseason before fading in the last two contests of the Western Conference final against the Chicago Blackhawks, losing the series 4–3.

Getzlaf was the first to recognize he did not play well

CAREER HIGHLIGHTS

Drafted 19th overall by the Anaheim Ducks in 2003

Member of Stanley Cup–winning Ducks in 2007

Ducks franchise leader with a plus-124

Nominated for the Mark Messier Leadership Award in 2014 and 2015

Recorded 208 goals and 678 points in 710 career games

in the last two games versus Chicago, finishing with a combined minus-4. Still, the only game in the series in which he didn't earn a single point was Game 6. And, much as they were in 2007, Getzlaf and Perry were a force in the postseason, particularly in their line with Patrick Maroon. Getzlaf also tied for the most assists in the playoffs with 18, despite not even playing in the final round.

Still riding high on their 2007 Cup win, Anaheim remains a top contender in the West, and as Getzlaf continues to shine, the team will likely remain secure in its success.

Oliver
EKMAN-LARSSON

Western Conference
Team Star

DEFENSE
23

goal from his own side of center ice to tie up the contest — a game Arizona went on to win 3–1 against the Maple Leafs. The goal was scored just five seconds into the third period, creating two records as it shot past Toronto goalie Jonathan Bernier. One, it tied the franchise record for the fastest goal to start a period (set by Doug Smail in 1981), and two, it became the fastest shorthanded goal to ever start an NHL period.

Secondly, two months later on the night of March 26, Ekman-Larsson scored against the Buffalo Sabres, marking his 21st goal of the season to become the first Swedish-born defenseman in the NHL to surpass the 20-goal mark.

Still not finished with the record books, Ekman-Larsson scored twice on April 4 against the San Jose Sharks in a 5–3 Arizona victory to give himself 23 goals on the season. That total equaled the franchise-high mark for defensemen, set by Phil Housley in 1991, when the team was located in Winnipeg.

Before any of this, however, Ekman-Larsson began his career with the Coyotes after they selected him sixth overall in the 2009 entry draft. His last full season playing in Sweden in 2009–10 saw the 6-foot-2, 190-pound defenseman score 33 points in 52 games, which was enough to catch the eye of the Coyotes. Ahead of the NHL, Ekman-Larsson recorded 10 points in 15 games for the San Antonio Rampage of the American Hockey League (AHL) before joining the Coyotes as a 19-year-old in 2010–11. The following season was his first full NHL campaign, in which he scored 13 goals, the most of any Arizona defenseman that season. The Coyotes ended up making the 2012 playoffs and got all the way to the third round (a franchise best) before being eliminated by the eventual Stanley Cup–winning Los Angeles Kings. The lockout-shortened season followed and Ekman-Larsson had a stellar 21 assists in all 48 games, which earned him some recognition as he came in seventh in votes for the James Norris Memorial Trophy that honors the best

A rizona Coyotes defenseman Oliver Ekman-Larsson had an excellent season in 2014–15. Unfortunately for him, it got lost in the wreckage of a poor year for the team. Arizona finished the season with the second-worst record of just 24 wins and 56 points. If Ekman-Larsson had played almost anywhere else in the league, he would have been recognized much more often as one of the best defensemen in the game, but because he toiled it out in the desert, he rarely received the recognition he deserved.

The Swedish-born defender was truly one of the lone bright spots in Arizona's dismal season. He scored 23 goals and 43 points, and had his share of career highlights along the way. Firstly, on the night of January 29, 2015, in Toronto, Ekman-Larsson scored a shorthanded

defenseman in the league. His last two seasons have been outstanding as he scored a combined 38 goals and 87 points. In 2014–15, Ekman-Larsson also scored seven game-winning goals (the highest mark on the Coyotes team), which indicates he is becoming a game changer who can turn it on when it matters.

A smooth skater, Ekman-Larsson is excellent at making the first pass out of his zone and can shut down the oppositions' best players. He became such a premier defenseman over the last two seasons that the Coyotes didn't hesitate to trade away top blue-liner Keith Yandle to the New York Rangers. The 24-year-old Ekman-Larsson has proven to be durable by skating over 25 minutes per game in each of his last three seasons. As he emerges as an elite defender, the opposition will naturally target him more, but Ekman-Larsson appears unfazed by the more physical demands his game has created.

The Coyotes have a batch of young players to add to their already youthful lineup, and fans can bet that Ekman-Larsson will be counted on to take even more of a leadership role. And, at only $5.5 million a season until 2019, the slick blue-liner might just be the best bargain in the NHL.

CAREER HIGHLIGHTS

Drafted 6th overall by the Arizona Coyotes in 2009

Led all NHL defensemen in 2014–15 in goals, game-winning goals and overtime goals

Finished fourth in 2014–15 for average time on ice among league defensemen playing all 82 games

Recorded 55 goals and 154 points in 340 career games

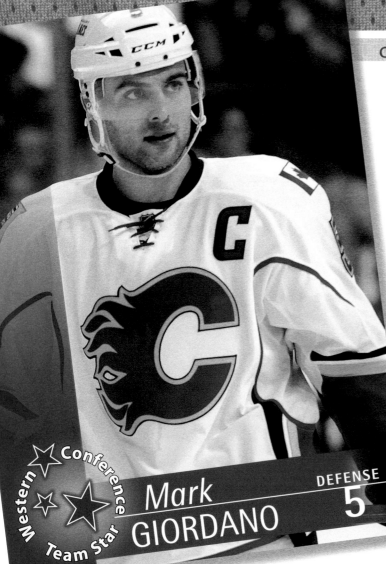

Western Conference Team Star

Mark GIORDANO

DEFENSE 5

he was 18 years old. The native of Toronto had played Junior A hockey for the Brampton Capitals of the Ontario Junior Hockey League (OJHL) in 2001–02, but he was not drafted by the NHL. Not wanting to give up, he accepted a tryout for the Owen Sound Attack of the Ontario Hockey League (OHL). Giordano was not overly large or highly skilled at that time, but Attack coach Mike Stothers, a former NHL defenseman, saw something in the raw blue-liner and gave him a spot on the team. Giordano stayed with Owen Sound for two full seasons and produced 97 points in 133 games.

Once his time with the Attack was over, the Flames signed Giordano as a free agent after inviting him to attend their summer camp. He spent the next three years developing in the American Hockey League (AHL), producing a 58-point season in 2005–06. He graduated to the Calgary club for 48 games in 2006–07, but he was hardly a star performer so the Flames let him go and he went to play in Russia for the Moscow Dynamo. Giordano stayed there for the full season in 2007–08, and although he only registered 12 points in 50 games, the 6-foot, 200-pound defender got plenty of ice time, thus improving all aspects of his game. Giordano's risky move paid off and he was back with the Flames the following year. By the time the 2009–10 season ended, he had scored 11 goals and totaled 30 points. The Flames soon locked him up with a five-year deal worth just over $20 million — not bad for an undrafted player.

Giordano's main strength is his ability to handle and move the puck. His passes are crisp and he is excellent on the attack, producing over 30 assists three times in his career to date. He is also valuable on the Flames' power play and has 98 career points with the extra man. Overall, his skating has improved immensely since the early days, and he is a first-rate team player who blocks shots when necessary and uses his body to protect the puck.

In addition to his all-round play, Giordano has

O n January 31, 2010, the Calgary Flames shocked their fans when they sent their best defenseman to the Toronto Maple Leafs. Dion Phaneuf had been drafted by the club ninth overall in 2003 and was supposed to lead the Calgary club for years to come. Many hockey experts didn't understand the deal, given that Phaneuf was only 24 years old and had already been a James Norris Memorial Trophy nominee. The Flames, however, had something of a secret weapon on their roster and his name was Mark Giordano, another young defenseman who soon made Calgary fans forget all about Phaneuf.

It is a remarkable story that Giordano is playing in the NHL at all, let alone so supported by the Flames organization, as his hockey career almost ended when

become the face of the Calgary franchise after being named team captain in 2013. He was a popular choice to wear the "C" on his sweater and was praised by head coach Bob Hartley for his strong leadership, work ethic and sacrifice for the team.

In Giordano's first season in Calgary, he had watched how Jarome Iginla — known for his kind heart and hard work — handled the captaincy role, and the former Flame proved to be the perfect role model for the younger Giordano.

The last two seasons have been great ones for Giordano who has combined totals of 25 goals and 95 points. These numbers have established him as one of the most valuable Flames players and one of the best defensemen in all of hockey. An injury in February 2015 ended his season, leaving him out of the Flames' resurgence into the playoffs entirely. If he can steer clear of injuries for the 2015–16 campaign, the 31-year-old should be able to enjoy some well-deserved postseason success.

CAREER HIGHLIGHTS

Led all Flames defensemen in goals, points and shots on goal in 2013–14

Averaged over 25 minutes played in 2013–14 and 2014–15

Played in his first NHL All-Star Game in 2015

Recorded 66 goals and 245 points in 510 career games

Western Conference Team Star

Jonathan
TOEWS

CENTER
19

team captain could do by devising a plan to recognize the lesser-known players who helped the team win it all again in 2015.

Known as "Captain Serious" since his early days as the Blackhawks' leader, Toews first joined Chicago after he was selected third overall in 2006. The 6-foot-2, 201-pound center had just finished high school at Shattuck-St. Mary's where he scored 110 points in 64 games. Toews then competed for Team Canada at the World Junior Championships in 2007 when the team won gold; Canadian fans can still recall his great performance when he scored three times in the shootout to seal victory against the Americans and gain a berth in the gold medal game.

Toews' first season with the Blackhawks came in 2007–08, and he scored 54 points in 64 games, finishing third in the race for the Calder Memorial Trophy for best rookie. That was the only season Toews has played with a Blackhawks team that didn't make the postseason.

From his rookie year through to 2014–15, Toews has been in the top-3 point scorers on his team every season except one. His offensive power has made him almost a point-per-game player, while his defensive skills have earned him one win and four Frank J. Selke Trophy nominations for best defensive forward in the NHL. His leadership on the ice was evident during the 2015 playoffs, especially when his team was at its breaking point. He scored two goals in Game 7 against the Anaheim Ducks in the third round and netted the key first goal against the Tampa Bay Lightning in Game 4 of the final round. The Blackhawks won that game and the next two to clinch the hard-fought series.

Toews' off-ice initiative was acknowledged with the 2015 Mark Messier Leadership Award for his participation in several charitable organizations. Toews is also the youngest member of the Triple Gold Club, having earned a Stanley Cup, an Olympic gold medal and a World Championship gold medal all by the age of 22.

The Chicago Blackhawks were anxiously awaiting the arrival of the Stanley Cup after they had just defeated the Tampa Bay Lightning to claim the NHL championship for the 2014–15 season. A terrible rainstorm in Chicago kept the Cup out of the building throughout Game 6 because a lot of the streets were flooded and impassable. When the Cup finally arrived, captain Jonathan Toews had the honor of accepting the award first — just the second time a Blackhawks captain had done so on home ice — before passing it to Kimmo Timonen, who had just played in his final NHL game. Then, as per Toews' instructions, Timonen passed the Cup to two players who were new to the team that season. A true leader thinks of others first, so it surprised no one when Toews did the classiest thing a

Ultimately, he is the perfect example of an all-around good person and great athlete.

Toews is a born leader who shows more by example than by words. He is a hard worker who won't stop until the buzzer brings an end to the game, and while he hasn't proven to be a prolific goal scorer, he has also never recorded less than 54 points in a full season. Others may put up higher numbers but no other current NHL captain has lifted the Stanley Cup three times like the 27-year-old native of Winnipeg, Manitoba, has already had the opportunity to do. Toews took the captaincy in February 2008 when he was just 20 years old and many wondered if he could handle the responsibility that comes with the "C." Considering all he has done, he handled it very well.

Toews is in elite company among captains with three Cup victories, and one more win, which seems very much in the realm of possibility, will put him on a short list that holds just six other names.

In 2014, the Blackhawks signed Toews to a new eight-year contract that will pay him an average annual salary of $10.5 million. In the eyes of management and fans alike, he is worth every dollar.

CAREER HIGHLIGHTS

Drafted 3rd overall by the Chicago Blackhawks in 2006

Three-time Stanley Cup winner with the Blackhawks (2010, 2013 and 2015)

Winner of the Conn Smythe Trophy in 2010

Recorded 39 goals and 102 points in 117 career playoff games

Recorded 223 goals and 506 points in 565 career games

Western Conference Team Star

Gabriel
LANDESKOG

LEFT WING
92

had ever given the honor to a European-born player. Landeskog responded with an even better year by scoring 36 times and totaling 66 points. At the time, hockey scouts saw the youngster as the most "NHL ready" player available for the 2011 entry draft, but despite the complimentary label, the Edmonton Oilers selected Ryan Nugent-Hopkins with the first pick of the draft, leaving Landeskog for the Colorado Avalanche, who selected him second overall. Edmonton's loss was Colorado's gain.

Landeskog was outstanding in his rookie year, scoring 22 goals (the most of any Colorado player that season) and recording 52 points in 82 games. Landeskog also took the top spot for games played, plus/minus rating and shots on goal. His terrific performance was rewarded with the Calder Memorial Trophy as the league's best rookie, and his season impressed the Avalanche so much that the 19-year-old was named team captain before the start of only his second NHL season. With this title, he became the youngest player to be named captain in league history. Landeskog described the experience as "something you dream about as a kid" and was honored to follow in the footsteps of former Avalanche captains Joe Sakic, Adam Foote and Milan Hejduk.

Just when things were going well, Landeskog suffered a concussion in the fourth game of his second campaign. He only played in 36 games of the 2012–13 lockout-shortened season, putting up just 17 points. Without their captain, Colorado sagged in the standings and a 48-game schedule left little time to gain a playoff spot. Luckily, Landeskog was able to return with a strong showing in 2013–14 and had his best year to date with 65 points (26 goals and 39 assists). The Avalanche team was also back in the playoffs for the first time since 2009–10, as they were guided by new coach and former Colorado goaltender Patrick Roy. Landeskog scored three goals in the opening-round playoff series against the Minnesota Wild, but an overtime loss in Game 7 ended Colorado's season. Over the last two seasons of

G abriel Landeskog's ability to adapt to North America has been remarkable considering he was born in Sweden and raised there until the age of 17. He started learning English in elementary school, but more importantly, he grew up playing a North American style of hockey. So when he arrived in Kitchener, Ontario, in 2009 to play junior hockey for the Kitchener Rangers, he was more than ready to take on the Ontario Hockey League (OHL).

The transition to major junior hockey in Canada went about as smoothly as it possibly could, with the 6-foot-1, 204-pound left-winger producing 46 points in 61 games during the 2009–10 season. Landeskog was so impressive that the Rangers made him team captain for the next season — the first time the junior team play, Landeskog has only missed one game, but was hurting during the 2014–15 campaign. He would never use an injury as an excuse, but had to have surgery in the offseason to correct a wrist problem. It forced him to miss the 2015 World Championships for the Swedish team, but he wanted to ensure he would be ready for the start of the 2015–16 NHL season.

One of the qualities that makes Landeskog a respected leader is the fact that he will do whatever it takes to win. When momentum has to swing toward his team, he is there with a hit or a fight (he has 231 penalty minutes in 288 career games, including the playoffs), and his ability to follow through with plays means he will be a good goal-scorer throughout his career. Overall, Landeskog tied with veteran Jarome Iginla for the most points on the team in

2014–15, and he is a career plus-35 at only 22 years old.

The ultra-competitive Landeskog has not maxed out his potential yet, as he leads a dynamic group of young Colorado players into the 2015–16 season. If the Avalanche can continue to improve under Roy, the team should flourish as playoff contenders in the years to come.

CAREER HIGHLIG

Drafted 2nd overall by the Colorado Avalanche in 2011

Winner of the Calder Memorial Trophy in 2011–12

Part of the First All-Rookie Team in 2011–12

Recorded 80 goals and 193 points in 281 career games

Western Conference Team Star

Tyler SEGUIN

CENTER
91

to immature off-ice behavior that didn't sit well with Bruins management (they said he underperformed during the 2013 playoffs, but his partying lifestyle is thought to be the real reason).

The Stars had recently hired Jim Nill as their new general manager and he was looking to significantly bolster his team's attack. Nill approached Boston boss Peter Chiarelli and the two managers negotiated a deal that sent four Stars (including Loui Eriksson and Reilly Smith) to the Bruins in exchange for Seguin and Rich Peverley. The Stars were thrilled to add a talent like Seguin — a young forward with excellent scoring power and a Stanley Cup under his belt.

From the moment of his arrival in the state of Texas, Seguin seemed to be a much more focused player and person. Firstly, he was back at center, whereas the Bruins often had him on the wing. Secondly, he found instant chemistry with another young Dallas player in team captain Jamie Benn. Thirdly, he had Lindy Ruff as a coach who was not going to stand for any nonsense. Indeed, it all came together for Seguin, who recorded 37 goals and 84 points in 2013–14, which was enough to finish fourth in league scoring. Dallas was quickly dispatched in the 2014 playoffs, but Seguin proved his numbers were no fluke when he came back in 2014–15 to record 77 points in 71 games played — a total that was good enough for second place in points per game, just behind Sidney Crosby. Seguin was also a top contender all season for the Art Ross Trophy (awarded for the most points in a season) until a knee injury from a hit by the Florida Panthers' Dmitry Kulikov knocked him out of the lineup for about a month. In Seguin's first game back, he scored two goals and finished the season strong, even though Dallas didn't make the playoffs.

This kind of perseverance and skill has been in development since Seguin joined the Stars. Over the seasons, his scoring abilities began to shine and the shot he had been practicing since he was five years old was perfected.

The past two seasons for Tyler Seguin have both been about proving his worth, as he was consistently touted early in his career as a potential NHL superstar. Drafted second overall by the Boston Bruins in 2010, the 6-foot-1, 205-pound native of Brampton, Ontario, joined an already stellar team that had acquired its high draft spot from the Toronto Maple Leafs via a trade for Phil Kessel. Seguin's first season saw him score 11 goals in 74 games with limited ice time. He also played in 13 postseason games, accumulated 7 points and helped the Bruins capture their first Stanley Cup since 1972. Following this, he put in two more good seasons with Boston, including 67 points in just his second NHL campaign, but was traded to the Dallas Stars for the start of the 2013–14 season due

He worked hard and kept goalies guessing as to what he would do with all the shots he loved to take (he has placed in the top 10 for shots on goal from 2012–13 to 2014–15). He also plays the game at breakneck speed while setting up plays for his teammates, having recorded 40 or more assists in each of his two years as a Star.

Unfortunately, Seguin didn't completely leave his off-ice issues behind in Boston. He was benched for the last game of the 2014–15 season after he was late for practice. Seguin was contrite about his mistake and accepted his punishment without complaint. He vowed to never let it happen again. At the same time, Seguin demonstrated his charitable side by starting his own foundation called

Seguin's Stars, which provides a luxury suite at every Dallas home game for people with spinal-cord injuries. Truly, if Seguin can just continue to focus on his game and stay grounded, there is no telling how much he will accomplish in the NHL.

CAREER HIGHLIGHTS

Drafted 2nd overall by the Boston Bruins in 2010

Member of the Bruins' Stanley Cup team in 2011

Led the Dallas Stars in goals in 2013–14 and 2014–15

Recorded 130 goals and 282 points in 354 career games

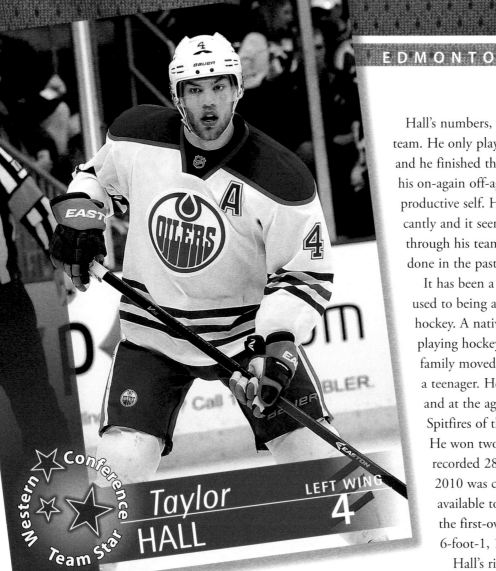

Western Conference Team Star

Taylor
HALL

LEFT WING
4

Hall's numbers, unfortunately, mirrored those of the team. He only played in 53 games because of injuries and he finished the year with just 38 points. Given his on-again off-again status, he wasn't his typical productive self. His shot attempts were down significantly and it seemed that he was unable to persevere through his team's poor performances as he had done in the past.

It has been a difficult time for Hall, who was used to being a winner in minor and junior hockey. A native of Calgary, Alberta, Hall began playing hockey on his backyard rink before his family moved to Kingston, Ontario, when he was a teenager. He continued to play minor hockey and at the age of 15 was selected by the Windsor Spitfires of the Ontario Hockey League (OHL). He won two Memorial Cups (2009 and 2010), recorded 280 points in three seasons and by 2010 was considered the best junior prospect available to be drafted. Edmonton secured the first-overall pick and happily added the 6-foot-1, 198-pound winger to their arsenal.

Hall's rise to NHL stardom hasn't come without its share of bumps. His game is built around his blazing speed and willingness to go to the net to score. It's an exciting style, but one that has translated into injury problems for the sniper, who has yet to suit up for a full NHL season. He's also had injuries of the freak kind — like when he fell during a pre-game warmup and had his forehead sliced open by a passing teammate's skate.

In 2014–15, his injuries were typical of his playing style — a sprained MCL in his right leg from a crash with the post led to a string of ankle and foot injuries. Hall is used to being out of the lineup for rehab, but it burned the crafty winger to watch the losses pile up for his team. Back on the active roster in March, Hall finished the year strong, with nine points in his last 12 games.

The former "City of Champions" (Edmonton councillors voted to remove the slogan from the city's

Taylor Hall's fifth season in the NHL was supposed to be a great one for him and his Edmonton Oilers teammates. The 2014–15 campaign was the second season for highly touted coach Dallas Eakins, who was set to improve the Oilers in his second year behind the bench. Hall was going to be counted upon to keep his offensive game alive — one that saw him net 80 points in 75 games the previous year — and be prominent on the attack with his young and potent linemates. Eakins, however, never got the team in gear and by the middle of December he was let go. Edmonton couldn't regain their footing either, finishing in the NHL's basement yet again. This also marked another year gone that Hall was with the Oilers but didn't make the playoffs.

welcome signs as the championships of the 1980s are long gone) is looking to regain its swagger. Loaded with talent from a bumper crop of high first-round draft picks that have come to the team by way of consistently terrible play, the Oilers have the right pieces in place. With players like Jordan Eberle, Ryan Nugent-Hopkins and Nail Yakupov, and a new general manager in Peter Chiarelli — who's not afraid to deal star players — it will be boom or bust for the Oilers.

With the No. 1 pick in 2015, the Oilers selected Connor McDavid, who is labeled as the next Sidney Crosby. They have also acquired goaltender Cam Talbot from the New York Rangers (career save percentage of .931), so heading into 2015–16, the sky seems the limit for the Edmonton club.

A win for Hall with Team Canada at the 2015 World Championships was a great relief for the winger, so if he can stay healthy and the Oilers can improve on the defensive side of the puck, the former No. 1 pick will certainly soon skate in his first NHL postseason game.

CAREER HIGHLIGHTS

Drafted 1st overall by the Edmonton Oilers in 2010

Recorded 50-plus points three times in the NHL

Finished in the league's top 10 in assists and points in 2012–13 and 2013–14

Recorded 106 goals and 263 points in 299 career games

Western Conference Team Star

Drew DOUGHTY

DEFENSE 8

many years to come because he has the right approach to the game, both mentally and physically. In the off-season, Doughty likes to rest and save something for the next year, since that will provide him with plenty of work to keep him in top condition. He plays a great deal during every game (including a career-high 28 minutes per contest and a league-leading 2,378 total ice time in 2014–15). In terms of his mental attitude, Doughty knows he can't be the perfect player on every shift, so mistakes slide off his back and he is able to come at the opponent with a force and determination to improve upon his errors. He rarely misses a game (only 16 in 7 seasons) and is one of the most reliable defense-men in the entire NHL — skills that earn him $7 million a season with the Kings.

The Kings selected Doughty second overall in the 2008 entry draft, just behind Steven Stamkos who went to the Tampa Bay Lightning. A native of London, Ontario, Doughty was already a Kings fan because of Wayne Gretzky, who had taken the time to respond to a fan letter from the Doughty household when he was playing in Los Angeles. Doughty was just six years old at the time, but Kings' paraphernalia and souvenirs started to appear in his bedroom, and eventually after a top junior career while playing for the Guelph Storm (157 points in 190 games), Los Angeles general manager Dean Lombardi paid a visit to Doughty's house before the 2008 draft. The Kings boss was impressed that the 6-foot-1, 213-pound defenseman was all about the team and not focused solely on his own personal achievements. The Kings needed a young defenseman to build around and Doughty was the man for the job.

The Kings missed the playoffs in Doughty's first season, but they came back fighting in 2009–10 and ended the season with 101 points, their best showing since 1990–91. Doughty contributed 59 points in 82 games, the most of any defenseman on the team. The Kings kept building by adding players like goalie

At the ripe old age of 25, Los Angeles Kings defenseman Drew Doughty has accomplished just about everything in professional hockey. He has won the Stanley Cup with the Los Angeles Kings twice (2012 and 2014) and is a two-time gold-medal winner of the Canadian men's hockey team at the Winter Olympics (2010 and 2014). He has been named a league All-Star (second team in 2009–10) and is a perennial candidate for the James Norris Memorial Trophy (awarded to NHL's best defenseman), finishing in the top three on two occasions, including the 2014–15 season. Outside of actually winning the coveted Norris, there is little left to achieve for the goofy yet tough blue-liner.

Doughty, however, will likely play pro hockey for

Jonathan Quick, center Anze Kopitar and winger Dustin Brown. The team was ready to make a statement by the time the 2012 playoffs began. Doughty chipped in 16 points in 20 playoff games as the Kings captured their first Stanley Cup in team history under coach Darryl Sutter, who joined the team late in the 2011–12 regular-season campaign. The Kings repeated their incredible performance in the 2014 playoffs, which included coming back from a 3–0 series deficit to the San Jose Sharks in the opening round. Doughty had 18 points in the playoffs as the Kings went on to edge out the Anaheim Ducks and Chicago Blackhawks before defeating the New York Rangers in five games for another Cup win.

Amazingly, the Kings missed the playoffs following the 2014–15 regular season, coming up four points short of the Winnipeg Jets. But Doughty was his usual self, chirping opposition players and weaving all over the ice with the puck dangling on the end of his stick.

Although Doughty's point production has never risen to the level of his second campaign, he continues to improve his game and strengthen his on-ice confidence as a valued member of the Kings' roster.

Western Conference Team Star

LEFT WING
11

Zach
PARISE

record, securing a playoff spot in the Western Conference with exactly 100 points. The team went on to defeat the tough St. Louis Blues in six games in the first round of the playoffs but were quickly eliminated by the Chicago Blackhawks in four straight games. It was made clear that the Wild will have to do much more to help Parise and Suter if they are to bring a Stanley Cup to the state of Minnesota, but the team's continuous improvements are signs of good things to come.

Parise had a great playoff run in 2015 with 10 points in 10 games. He also played a big role in knocking out the Blues with three goals and four assists in the series. Ultimately, though, it was another disappointing postseason for the 30-year-old, who has appeared in the playoffs a total of nine times in his career but has never been able to win the Stanley Cup. He came close in 2012 with the New Jersey Devils (the team that drafted him), but the Los Angeles Kings took them out in the final round. After that season, Parise signed a 13-year, $98-million contract with the Wild, hoping his new team would be the one to help him win the Cup.

Parise isn't a large man at 5-foot-11 and 190 pounds, but he is the ultimate competitor. Much like his father, there is no quit in his play — he has six seasons with over 60 points, including 94 in 2008–09 for fifth place in the league. Injuries have slowed him down since he went to the Wild and he has missed significant time over the last two seasons, but the relentless Parise managed a team-high 33 goals and 62 points in 74 games while he worked on a line with Mikael Granlund and Jason Pominville in 2014–15. This campaign marked the sixth time in Parise's career that he scored 30 or more goals, which shows just how consistent and valuable he is to his team. If the Wild can secure more offensive help, then some of the pressure to perform may come off Parise's shoulders, allowing him to be even more productive on the ice.

When Zach Parise signed as a free agent with the Minnesota Wild in 2012, he felt it was the right move. The left-winger was coming back to the state where he was born, along with his good friend Ryan Suter, and Parise became even more certain he had made the right decision when, during the 2014–15 season, his father Jean-Paul was dying of lung cancer. Jean-Paul had been a long-time NHL player and was one of the best in the history of the Minnesota North Stars between 1967 and 1974. When he died in January 2015, Zach was with him in his final days, but he only missed a handful of games, returning to his team to participate in the race to the playoffs.

After acquiring goalie Devan Dubnyk halfway through the season, the Wild finished with a 28–9–3

The smooth-skating winger is highly respected throughout the NHL for his strong work ethic. He will do whatever it takes to win, including hustling for rebounds around the opposition's net or blocking a shot in his own end of the ice. Parise is also exceptionally good on the power play and has led the Wild over the past three seasons in goals with the extra man for a total of 32.

Parise is not one to take a shift off and that brings a great deal of energy to his teammates, who feed off his great efforts. He is also the type of leader who molds his team into better players — an invaluable trait in the world of today's NHL.

Parise's biggest job going forward, however, will be to lead his team past the second round of the playoffs, and that is a task his personality relishes and playing style is suited to.

CAREER HIGHLIGHTS

Drafted 17th overall by the New Jersey Devils in 2003

Named to the NHL's Second All-Star Team for the 2008–09 season

Minnesota Wild franchise leader in playoff points with 25

Recorded 274 goals and 566 points in 691 career games

Western Conference
Team Star

Shea
WEBER

DEFENSE
6

In July 2012, the Philadelphia Flyers tried to solve one of their biggest problems by giving the largest offer sheet in NHL history to restricted free agent and Nashville Predator Shea Weber. The Flyers were in need of a dominating defenseman after Chris Pronger was forced to stop playing the year before and the team believed a big offer (14 years with a total value of $110 million) to the 6-foot-4, 220-pound Weber would scare off Nashville from matching the contract. The Predators, however, had already lost high-end blue-liner Ryan Suter to the Minnesota Wild as an unrestricted free agent so they were not about to let their captain leave. Even though the Predators are not considered a big-market team, they had to make a statement to their fans and to the rest of the hockey world that they were here to

compete. So the offer sheet was matched and Weber will now most likely be a Predator for the rest of his hockey career.

The fact that such staggering numbers were being tossed Weber's way was remarkable for the 49th draft pick in 2003. The native of Sicamous, British Columbia, had flown well under the radar while playing junior hockey for the Kelowna Rockets of the Western Hockey League (WHL). He played in the shadow of the more highly regarded defensemen Duncan Keith and Josh Gorges, but eventually caught the eye of Nashville scouts, even though his numbers were less than impressive (he scored only two goals in 2002–03). Still, the Predators made Weber the fourth player they chose in the 2003 entry draft and have never regretted the decision.

After playing most of the 2005–06 season for the Milwaukee Admirals of the American Hockey League (AHL), Weber played his first full season in Nashville the following year, recording 40 points in 79 games. Since then, Weber has become one of the most dominating defensemen in all of hockey and has been nominated for the James Norris Memorial Trophy three times, including two runner-up finishes in 2011 and 2012. Those same two seasons saw Weber earn First All-Star Team recognition due to his constant improvement.

Not only is Weber a superstar performer, he is also one of the most feared players in the NHL. That fear is not because he is a rough player, but is based on the fact that he has one of the most devastating slap shots in the league. Weber first started developing his shot as a young boy when he would blast away at plywood; he would also find empty cans to use as targets, and all of this practice has certainly paid off. His shot was clocked at a leading 108.5 miles per hour during the 2015 NHL All-Star Skills Competition, which was second overall to Boston Bruins defenseman Zdeno Chara, who recorded 108.8 miles per hour in 2012. No one wants to get in

front of Weber's drive — just ask former Detroit Red Wings goalie Chris Osgood, who "survived" a slap shot to the head by the big blue-liner in 2010.

Weber's great shot has allowed him to score double-digit goals seven times, lead his fellow Nashville defensemen in shots on goal since he joined the team full time in 2006–07 and sit in third place in franchise history for points, goals and assists. He is also fantastic on the power play, recording 161 career points with the extra man and having a rating of plus-55 (another franchise record).

The Predators had one of their best seasons in team history in 2014–15 (47 wins and 104 points), but once again failed to do much in the playoffs. The Chicago Blackhawks eliminated Nashville in six games, with Weber suffering a leg injury that limited him to the first two games of the series. It

was clear the Predators missed their captain. Going forward, though, Weber has a good group of defensemen to work with (Seth Jones, Roman Josi and Ryan Ellis), which will ease the pressure on him so he can fully recover and get back to his dominating ways.

CAREER HIGHLIGHTS

Drafted 49th overall by the Nashville Predators in 2003

Led all defensemen in 2013–14 in goals (23)

Holds the record for most power-play goals (66) in Predators history

Recorded 146 goals and 392 points in 685 career games

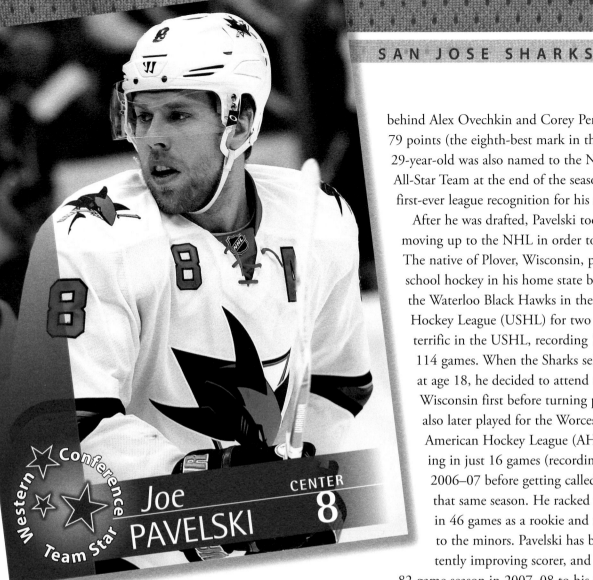

Western Conference Team Star

Joe
PAVELSKI

CENTER
8

behind Alex Ovechkin and Corey Perry) and recorded 79 points (the eighth-best mark in the NHL). The 29-year-old was also named to the NHL's Second All-Star Team at the end of the season, marking his first-ever league recognition for his superior talents.

After he was drafted, Pavelski took his time moving up to the NHL in order to hone his skills. The native of Plover, Wisconsin, played high school hockey in his home state before playing for the Waterloo Black Hawks in the United States Hockey League (USHL) for two seasons. He was terrific in the USHL, recording 121 points in 114 games. When the Sharks selected Pavelski at age 18, he decided to attend the University of Wisconsin first before turning professional. He also later played for the Worcester Sharks of the American Hockey League (AHL), participating in just 16 games (recording 26 points) in 2006–07 before getting called up to San Jose that same season. He racked up 28 points in 46 games as a rookie and never returned to the minors. Pavelski has been a consistently improving scorer, and from his first full 82-game season in 2007–08 to his most recent in 2014–15, Pavelski has gone from 40 to 70 points — not bad for a seventh-round pick.

A nose for the net and a quick, accurate shot are some of the attributes Pavelski displays on a nightly basis. In 2013–14 and 2014–15, he was the Sharks' top goal scorer, as well as in possession of the highest shooting percentage for anyone playing the full season. His high number of shots on goal helped him to score a league-best 44 goals during the calendar year of 2014, which was two more than Rick Nash and Tyler Seguin, who both scored 42 times. Former Sharks coach Todd McLellan has noted that Pavelski can score in a variety of ways, including deflections, tip-ins and rebounds, meaning he is not afraid to go to the net and take a beating if it means getting a goal for his team.

Pavelski's skill hasn't gone unnoticed. Named to the U.S. Olympic team for the 2014 Winter Games, he

W hen the San Jose Sharks drafted center Joe Pavelski in the seventh round of the 2003 entry draft, not much was expected of the 5-foot-11, 190-pound prospect. Players selected that late in the draft are generally not considered to have a lot of NHL potential. Every so often, however, a late-round pick will rise up and show that he should have been considered sooner. Pavelski is one of those players.

Since joining the Sharks in 2006, Pavelski has been a steady and consistent producer, but nobody could have anticipated his breakout season in 2013–14. His performance not only made him one of the top players on the Sharks team, but it elevated him to becoming one of the best players in the league. By the time the season was over, Pavelski had scored 41 times (the third-best total played on a line with Phil Kessel and James van Riemsdyk and had five points in six games. However, just like in his NHL career, Pavelski has yet to be on an international team that has won a medal or championship.

The Sharks are still recovering from their shocking 2014 playoff loss to the Los Angeles Kings after being up three games to none. San Jose didn't even make the postseason in 2015, the first time that has happened since 2002–03. Thus, Sharks management wants to steer the leadership of the team toward players like Pavelski and Logan Couture, and away from veterans like Joe Thornton and Patrick Marleau. Going into 2015–16, perhaps new head coach Peter DeBoer will give the Sharks and their younger players a new perspective that will get them back into the postseason and to the Stanley Cup final — after all, a championship for Pavelski would be a crowning achievement for an accomplished player who came out of nowhere to become a force to be reckoned with.

Vladimir
TARASENKO

RIGHT WING
91

Western Conference Team Star

the team's 14th choice in the 2010 entry draft. The Blues had made plans to draft Jaden Schwartz, a top prospect from the Tri-City Storm of the United States Hockey League (USHL) no matter what happened with Tarasenko, but he was such a tantalizing pick that the team could only dream of landing both players. St. Louis believed the two youngsters could be the best combination on the Blues since the days of Adam Oates and Brett Hull (both Hall of Fame players). The only concern was that Tarasenko might not even want to come to North America, opting instead to play at home in the Kontinental Hockey League (KHL) like many other native Russian players.

When the ninth pick came and went without Tarasenko being selected, Armstrong started to make some calls and found out that the Ottawa Senators were interested in Blues defenseman David Rundblad. With a deep blue-line already in place, St. Louis made the swap, took Schwartz with the 14th pick and then Tarasenko with what was supposed to be the Senators' pick at 16th overall. Tarasenko knew some teams had strong reservations about picking Russian-born players and was therefore pleased to pull on a St. Louis sweater, all the while hoping he could help get the team back into playoff contention.

To start off, Tarasenko did go back home to play in the KHL, but he returned to North America to play for the Blues to start the 2012–13 lockout-shortened season. He appeared in 38 games and scored eight times but upped that total to 21 the following year when he played in 64 games, showing glimpses of what he could do. Then came 2014–15 when Tarasenko really became a showstopper.

He was almost a point-per-game player with 73 points in 77 games, and he led the Blues with 37 goals, a rating of plus-27 and 264 shots on goal. He tied in third in the league for even-strength goals and came in sixth for goals per game. Tarasenko scored more than his fair share of highlight-reel goals in which he puckhandled

Willingness to go to the net is one thing — it's a high-risk, physical play and those who do it often pay the price — but players like the St. Louis Blues' right-winger Vladimir Tarasenko, who are blessed with soft hands, patience and a knack for finding holes in goalies, feel that in front of the net is exactly where they should be.

It seemed like the entire 2014–15 season was a highlight reel for the stocky 6-foot, 219-pound Tarasenko who scored one beautiful goal after another. He broke out with 37 goals in 77 games and added six markers in six playoff games. His performances put the league on notice that a new sniper was on the prowl.

Blues general manager Doug Armstrong had his eyes on Tarasenko and was hoping he would be available for

through players and then deked the goalie. His most famous play came in 2014 against the New York Rangers and goaltender Henrik Lundqvist. Tarasenko flew down from center ice, split the defense and put the puck in the net with only one hand on his stick.

When Tarasenko wasn't going coast-to-coast on a rush, he would whip a terrific snap-shot to light the lamp. His big body also allowed him to absorb a lot of hits and he had no trouble succeeding when the game got physical. Tarasenko is a clean player, however, and he only has 57 career penalty minutes (with none in the playoffs), instead using his natural skill to make room for himself on the ice.

All in all, the three years Tarasenko stayed in Russia before coming to St. Louis were worth the wait. The team won 51 games and recorded 109 points in 2014–15 for first place in the Central Division. These numbers proved

the squad is well balanced, but a playoff loss in the first round to the Minnesota Wild likely made Tarasenko and his teammates that much more hungry for success in the seasons to come.

CAREER HIGHLIGHTS

Drafted 16th overall by the St. Louis Blues in 2010

Played in the 2015 NHL All-Star Game

Named one of the NHL Stars of the Month in November 2014

Named to the NHL's Second All-Star Team in 2015

Recorded 66 goals and 135 points in 179 career games

Western Conference Team Star

Daniel SEDIN

LEFT WING 22

came up about the Sedins' abilities, but there is no denying the talent the brothers possess.

It should be noted that Daniel did not have his most productive playoff run, with only 4 points and a minus-1 rating. The twins also faced the brunt of the Game 6 loss after Vancouver built up a 3–0 lead less than 10 minutes into the contest, yet managed to lose 7–4. At 34 years old, however, the Sedins still managed to prove they have plenty left in the tank. Linden and Benning have conceded they want to make roster changes via trades, which might mean asking players like Daniel and Henrik to waive their no-trade clauses, but it's more likely that they will remain in Vancouver for the rest of their careers and will mentor top prospects like Jake Virtanen, Jared McCann, Hunter Shinkaruk and Cole Cassels.

Many were surprised the Canucks decided to sign the twins to new four-year contracts worth $28 million after a rather dismal showing in 2013–14, when Daniel collected only 47 points and Henrik earned just slightly more with 50. Throw in the debacle with coach John Tortorella, whose intense style did not suit the Sedins (he misused their skills) and it seemed like a possibility that the Sedins might not even want to stay on the west coast with a squad that missed the playoffs for the first time in five years. But stay they did, and the brothers led the team back to respectability in 2014–15 while Daniel produced one of his best all-round seasons since joining the NHL. He finished eighth in the league in points, third in assists and combined with his brother for 50 power-play points.

Daniel was drafted by the Canucks in 1999 (second overall while Henrik went third after some exhaustive maneuvering by then–general manager Brian Burke to get both), and the 6-foot-1, 187-pound left-winger has been a consistent and productive performer ever since. He has scored 327 goals and 881 points in 1,061 games, with his best mark being a league-leading 104 points in 2010–11. In 14 seasons, he has had only three with less

The 2014–15 season began with plenty of new faces on the Vancouver Canucks' executive team. Former players Trevor Linden and Jim Benning took over the management reins and Willie Desjardins signed on to be behind the bench after a successful career in the American Hockey League (AHL). Two faces that didn't change, however, were those of team leaders and twin brothers Daniel and Henrik Sedin. Daniel led the team in points with 76 (20 goals and 56 assists), followed by Henrik with 73. They were also the only two Canucks who played in all 82 games. The team put together a 48–29–5 record, good enough for 101 points and a playoff spot. They faced their division-rival Calgary Flames in the postseason, and when the Flames took the series in six games, the usual questions than 40 points (not even including the lockout-shortened season of 2012–13), and he now leads the Canucks in all-time power-play goals, game-winning goals and shots on goal. Sedin is not only a smart hockey player, but he also has incredibly soft hands. He is able to dangle with the puck and keep the opposition guessing as to what he is going to do next. His on-ice chemistry with his brother is also still sharp, and if anyone were to question Daniel or Henrik's dedication to winning, they should consider that the brothers' career plus/minus numbers show plus-177 and plus-214, respectively.

Daniel and Henrik are consummate team players and in the coming seasons will be able to prove their veteran status as they provide younger Canucks with assistance and advice. The team is now transitioning under Desjardins, with high hopes of taking home the franchises's first-ever Stanley Cup, and if the Canucks accomplish this ultimate goal, Daniel and Henrik are sure to be at the heart of the achievement.

CAREER HIGHLI...

Drafted 2nd overall by the Vancouver Canucks in 1999

Winner of the 2011 Art Ross Trophy and the Ted Lindsay Award

Part of the NHL First All-Star Team for the 2010–11 season

Recorded 327 goals and 881 points in 1,061 career games

Western Conference Team Star

Dustin
BYFUGLIEN

DEFENSE/
RIGHT WING
33

games. His cross-check to the back of the head of New York Rangers forward J.T. Miller was a vicious assault that cost Byfuglien a four-game suspension just as the Jets were trying to secure a playoff spot. Luckily, his team made up for his absence and continued into the postseason against the Anaheim Ducks. In Game 3 of the series, the lesser version of Byfuglien came out again and sucker-punched Corey Perry after he scored a goal. There was no suspension this time, but the Ducks swept the Jets, and the Winnipeg team is now left to wonder which side of the enigmatic Byfuglien will show up for the 2015–16 season and beyond.

Byfuglien was raised by his mother in Minnesota, where they lived in a trailer behind his grandparents' house. He began taking an interest in hockey when he got a used pair of skates and a hockey stick that he paid for bit by bit. His mother encouraged him to continue his hockey career when it looked like he might give it up, and as a result sent the 16-year-old to Chicago to play minor hockey. He eventually caught the eye of junior scouts when he scored 142 points in 189 games during his time in the Western Hockey League (WHL) playing for the Brandon Wheat Kings and Prince George Cougars between 2001 and 2005.

He was by no means considered a highly touted prospect, but the Chicago Blackhawks took a chance on him in the eighth round of the 2003 entry draft. Byfuglien was again having doubts about his passion to play professional hockey, but on he went to the Norfolk Admirals of the American Hockey League (AHL) for development. He was successful with the Admirals, recording 67 points in 116 games over two seasons. Denis Savard was coaching the Blackhawks at the time and decided to convert Byfuglien into a power forward for the 2007–08 season, which ended up being the ideal role for the right-winger.

During the 2009–10 regular season, Byfuglien scored 17 goals and 17 assists, but was especially good in the

D uring the 2014–15 season, the enigmatic Dustin Byfuglien continued to confuse the hockey world. One version of the Winnipeg Jets player was fit, focused and used his 6-foot-5, 265-pound frame to dominate the physical aspects of the game. His experience as both a defenseman and a forward had created the perfect player. He could intimidate his opponents by playing on the edge of the rulebook while simultaneously scoring 45 points in 69 games. His work while manning the point on the power play was also excellent, recording 17 power-play points, which proved he could score as well as set up his teammates with the extra man.

The other version of Byfuglien was not in the best condition in 2014–15. He tired easily, causing him to take foolish penalties that hurt his team's chances to win

playoffs when Chicago met the Vancouver Canucks. Playing like a linebacker on skates, he scored a hat trick during Game 3 of the series, helping to close out the Canucks in six games. Byfuglien had 16 points in 22 playoff games and the Blackhawks took home the Stanley Cup for the first time since 1961. Chicago was then forced to make changes because of salary-cap issues and the emerging Byfuglien was sent to the Atlanta Thrashers. He had a great season as a Thrasher, recording a then-career-high of 53 points before moving with the team to Winnipeg.

Byfuglien had a career-best 56 points in 2013–14 and played in 78 games. He has been in the top 5 for both points and penalty minutes during four seasons in Winnipeg and one in Atlanta. He has played in two All-Star games (2011 and 2015) and seemed like an unstoppable force for the Jets in 2014–15 when he

notched a career-high 124 penalty minutes. If Byfuglien can learn to control his power and harness it for offensive attacks, the Jets might be able to make the postseason in 2015–16 with a player who is less of an enigma and more of a finely tuned weapon.

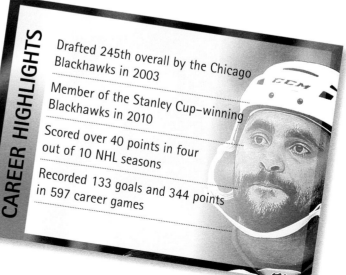

CAREER HIGHLIGHTS

Drafted 245th overall by the Chicago Blackhawks in 2003

Member of the Stanley Cup–winning Blackhawks in 2010

Scored over 40 points in four out of 10 NHL seasons

Recorded 133 goals and 344 points in 597 career games

MASKED MARVELS

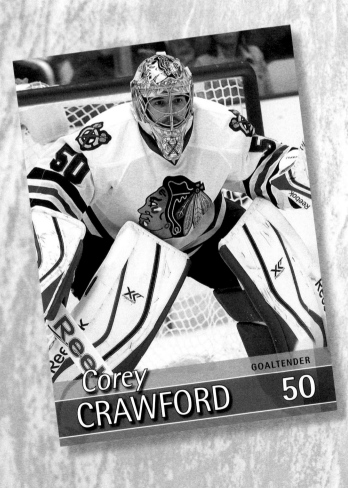

Ben BISHOP

Corey CRAWFORD
GOALTENDER
50

Tuukka RASK
GOALTENDER
40

Ryan
MILLER
GOALTENDER
30

Marc-Andre
FLEURY
GOALTENDER
29

Braden
HOLTBY

Pekka
RINNE
GOALTENDER
35

Jonathan
QUICK
GOALTENDER
32

League (NAHL) for the 2004–05 season in which he won 35 of the 45 games he played. The Blues drafted the hometown kid 85th overall at the 2005 entry draft, but Bishop went to the University of Maine for the next three years, finishing with a 2.29 goals-against average.

Once his college career came to a close, Bishop was assigned to the Peoria Rivermen of the American Hockey League (AHL) for the next three seasons. His solid play, however, wasn't enough to earn him a regular spot with the St. Louis Blues (he appeared in only 13 games over two seasons), so he was dealt to the Ottawa Senators in February 2012. At the time, Bishop was one of the best goalies in the AHL, but he served to merely back up Craig Anderson until he returned from an injury. Meanwhile, the Tampa Bay Lightning were not happy with their goaltending and general manager Steve Yzerman made a deal to acquire Bishop in April 2013, giving up very little to acquire the large netminder. Bishop's first full season in Tampa (2013–14) was his best ever. He had a 37–14–7 record, a .924 save percentage, a 2.23 goals-against average and five shutouts. He was nominated for the Vezina Trophy for best goaltender and got the Lightning back to the playoffs for the first time in three years. Unfortunately, Bishop was hurt toward the end of the regular season and the necessary surgery forced him to miss the postseason. As a result, the team was swept by the Montreal Canadiens.

Bishop came back even stronger in 2014–15, winning 40 games and helping his team to earn 108 points for their best finish in franchise history. The Lightning got past three Original Six teams in the playoffs, including goaltenders Carey Price of the Montreal Canadiens and Henrik Lundqvist of the New York Rangers, who are two of the best goalies in the league. It was a tough road to the final round, having played 20 games to get there, but the Lightning were on a roll when they faced the Chicago Blackhawks for the Cup. Bishop tore a

Ben BISHOP

GOALTENDER 30

At 6-foot-7, Ben Bishop is one of the tallest goaltenders to ever play in the NHL. Few experts would have predicted that such a large man could be an effective netminder in the fast-moving game of hockey, but Bishop has proven to be one of the best, and in the 2015 playoffs he took the Tampa Bay Lightning all the way to the Stanley Cup final (their last time getting that far was in 2004 when they won the Cup).

Bishop was born in Denver, Colorado, but grew up in St. Louis, Missouri. He started to play hockey as a forward in the St. Louis area, but turned to goaltending in order to stay on the ice for the entire game. He played AAA hockey in St. Louis before joining the Texas Tornado of the North American Hockey

groin muscle during this final series, but he still played in five of six games, fighting through the pain. It wasn't enough, though, and Tampa Bay fell to Chicago.

Overall, Bishop's game is not always technically sound, nor is his movement as quick as that of other goalies, but he always seems to come out on top when challenged to do so. In the 2014–15 postseason, his numbers were great with a .921 save percentage, 2.18 goals-against average and a league-leading three shutouts. His superior puckhandling skills also annoy the opposition because he can make great breakout passes and has even assisted on six goals in his career.

At 28 years old, Bishop is in the prime of his hockey career, but with backup goalie Andrei Vasilevskiy proving his worth, he needs to stay healthy and continue to improve in the crease if he wants to stay there. As it stands, Bishop has the opportunity to not only become one of Tampa Bay's best goaltenders, but one of the greatest in the NHL.

Drafted 85th overall by the St. Louis Blues in 2005

Placed fourth in wins in 2013–14 and 2014–15

Leads all Lightning goaltenders with a .920 save percentage and a 2.32 goals-against average

Posted a 95–44–16 record in 170 career games

CAREER HIGHLIGHTS

GOALTENDER

Corey
CRAWFORD 50

American Hockey League (AHL), where he spent five long years. He had 135 AHL wins to his credit, but a chance with the Blackhawks was proving to be elusive. He finally caught a break just after Chicago won the Stanley Cup in 2010. Goaltender Antti Niemi left for the San Jose Sharks due to salary-cap restraints, opening up a spot for Crawford in the Windy City.

Crawford won 63 games over his first two seasons in the Chicago net, but two early playoff exits trumped his success. Determined to prove his worth, Crawford went 19–5–5 during the lockout-shortened season of 2012–13 and led the Blackhawks to a first-place finish with 77 points. His stellar season won him the William M. Jennings Trophy for fewest goals scored against. Crawford also led during the postseason with 16 wins and a 1.84 save percentage on the way to Chicago's second Cup in four years. It wasn't an easy triumph for the Blackhawks, and the Boston Bruins had them on the ropes in the final round, but Crawford found a way to bounce back.

His reputation of doing just enough to win started during that series and while it is not always pretty, Crawford is now known as a champion. Following this season, he signed a six-year, $36-million contact, indicating that he had truly made it in the NHL.

Like many other goalies of the modern game, Crawford is a large player at 6-foot-2 and 208 pounds. There is not a lot of graceful movement in his play, but he covers the bulk of the net with his size and tries to be in a good position to use his frame to his advantage. And, while he can be a little slow to cover up loose pucks, he never quits on a play, especially when his team needs a big save.

In 2014–15, Crawford won 32 games and, in a full season, had the fewest goals allowed of his career. The 2015 playoffs, on the other hand, didn't start well for Crawford, who was replaced by backup Scott Darling during the opening series versus the Nashville

Two of the best words to describe Chicago Blackhawks goaltender Corey Crawford are "dedication" and "tenacity." It certainly hasn't been easy for Crawford to climb to the top of the NHL, but slowly and surely he has added his name to the list of the top netminders in the NHL today, and if he keeps playing the way he has, he will soon rate as one of the best of all time.

A native of Montreal, Quebec, Crawford was selected by Chicago in the second round of the 2003 entry draft. He played junior hockey for the Moncton Wildcats of the Quebec Major Junior Hockey League (QMJHL) and sported a record of 96–68–18 over four seasons. When his junior career was over, Crawford was assigned to the Norfolk Admirals and Rockford IceHogs in the

Predators. If Chicago coach Joel Quenneville was sending Crawford a message, it was certainly received, as he came back to win the 12 required victories in the next three rounds to claim the Stanley Cup. Crawford made the big saves at the right times (Tampa Bay Lightning superstar Steven Stamkos didn't score one goal against Crawford in the final round), and Crawford finished Game 6 with a 2–0 shutout in front of the hometown fans in Chicago for the Blackhawks' first championship victory

on home ice in 77 years. Not only had Crawford won his second Stanley Cup, but he also earned his second William M. Jennings Trophy.

In the upcoming seasons, the Blackhawks will face many financial decisions and it may turn out that Crawford will have to leave like Niemi did a few years ago, but if that happens, the 30-year-old will not be unemployed for long, as many other teams would love to benefit from Crawford's Stanley Cup–winning ways.

CAREER HIGHLIGHTS

Drafted 52nd overall by the Chicago Blackhawks in 2003

Two-time winner of the Stanley Cup and William M. Jennings Trophy (2013 and 2015)

Leads all Chicago goalies with 45 wins in 76 playoff games

Posted a 147–79–34 record in 268 career games

Marc-Andre FLEURY

GOALTENDER

29

Marc-Andre Fleury was just 24 years old in 2009 when he won the Stanley Cup as the goaltender for the Pittsburgh Penguins. He made a heart-stopping save in the final seconds of Game 7 to give the club its first championship since 1992. It was assumed that this was just the start of postseason success for the Peguins because of players like Fleury, Sidney Crosby, Kris Letang and Evgeni Malkin, but things haven't worked out that way and most of the blame has fallen on the goaltender — the common scapegoat for unsuccessful teams — even though Fleury is one of the NHL's best netminders.

Fleury holds several franchise records, including games played (595), wins (322), save percentage (.911), goals-against average (2.59) and shutouts (38). His

2014–15 season was also one of redemption as he posted a 34–20–9 record, came in eighth in the league with 1,685 saves and led the NHL with 10 shutouts. His save percentage (playing at least 40 games) was a career-best .920 and his 2.32 goals-against average tied his best mark that he first established in 2010–11. His teammates were also constantly noting that it was Fleury who was keeping them alive for most of the season (the Penguins squeaked into the playoffs with 98 points) and that the acrobatic goalie was really the most valuable player on the team.

Fleury is not perfect, though, and he does deserve some criticism when looking at the team's misses over the last few seasons. Take, for example, the 2012 playoffs when the Penguins met the Philadelphia Flyers in the first round. Pittsburgh had won 51 games in the regular season and had racked up 108 points, making them the clear favorite over their state rivals. Fleury, however, gave up 26 goals in the six-game series and the Flyers continued on to the second round while the Penguins were left to lick their wounds. It seems that Fleury hasn't been able to fully shake that performance and has used the services of a sports psychologist to try and move on. He also tries to keep improving by watching a lot of video footage and working with Pittsburgh goaltending coach Mike Bales.

Pittsburgh's general manager Jim Rutherford (a former NHL goaltender himself) liked what he saw in Fleury's approach to his job and wanted to give him some security with a new contract in 2014. Many were calling for Pittsburgh to look at other options in goal and to consider trading the 30-year-old Fleury, but Rutherford remained steadfast and gave his netminder a four-year deal worth $23 million. Penguins coach Mike Johnston, a rookie bench boss in 2014–15, also recognized Fleury's need for a mental break and gave him days off to help ease the pressure and demands of the job. This tactic worked in the regular season, but the Penguins were too worn down to be a factor in the playoffs and the New

York Rangers dispensed the Pittsburgh club in just five games.

Despite the bad ending to the playoffs, Fleury has shown that he is a fighter who will not easily give up his crease. It's the same approach he has used since the Penguins drafted him first overall in 2003, but over time Fleury has been able to refine his game to the point where he is calmer in his net and not so reliant on his superb reflexes. When he needs it, though, his glove hand is one of the fastest in the league and has left many goal scorers shaking their heads in disbelief.

With a new contract secured, Fleury can continue to improve his game without the worry of a trade. The Penguins, however, will need to create more offense in order to make Fleury's job easier, which will in turn give the team a shot at getting back to the Stanley Cup final.

Drafted 1st overall by the Pittsburgh Penguins in 2003

Stanley Cup winner in 2009 with the Penguins

Has won 34-plus games 7 times in 11 NHL seasons

Led the NHL in shutouts in 2014–15, with 10

Posted a 322–189–55 record in 595 career games

CAREER HIGHLIGHTS

Braden
HOLTBY

GOALTENDER

70

smooth transition into the top goalie spot on the Capitals team. The 2013–14 season was a tough one for the native of Lloydminster, Saskatchewan. Head coach Adam Oates and goalie coach Olaf Kolzig (a former star netminder for the Capitals) tried to change Holtby's style and the results were disastrous. He posted a respectable record of 23–15–4 with a save percentage of .915, but he struggled with his confidence and his team missed the playoffs. Oates and Kolzig preferred a more conservative approach to goaltending, which went against Holtby's natural abilities. At one point, the Capitals even acquired veteran Jaroslav Halak in a desperate bid to make the playoffs, but when that didn't happen, the team knew it ultimately had to rely on Holtby.

The Capitals' failure to appear in the post-season meant the end of the line for Oates, which made way for Barry Trotz to take over. Trotz had been a long-time coach with the Nashville Predators and he brought along his own goalie coach when he moved to the Capitals. Mitch Korn, a 16-year veteran at coaching netminders, was much easier for Holtby to deal with since they both shared the same mental approach to the position. Trotz and Korn worked to get Holtby to see the puck more and stay calm under pressure. They emphasized Holtby's natural athletic skills and taught him to be more efficient with his movements. They also put Holtby in a better position to face shots and showed him how to use his great glove hand to maximum advantage.

Holtby responded well to his new teachers, as evidenced by his 2014–15 campaign. He played in a league-leading 73 games, finished second in wins with 41 (just one behind Carey Price) and recorded a career-high nine shutouts. His save percentage went up to .923 and his goals-against average was an excellent 2.22. Holtby also got the Capitals back into the playoffs where they won the first round against the New York Islanders before losing to the New York Rangers in seven games,

Back in 2010–11, the Washington Capitals featured three goaltenders in their lineup, none older than 22 years of age. The trio split the entire season for the Capitals, combining for a total of 48 victories. Michal Neuvirth played in 48 games while Semyon Varlamov played in 27. The youngest of the trio was Braden Holtby, who was just 21 years old at the time. He only played in 14 games, but posted a 10–2–2 record, which was the best ratio between the three goaltenders. By the 2014–15 season, both Neuvirth and Varlamov had been dispatched from the Capitals (traded to the Buffalo Sabres and Colorado Avalanche, respectively), and these exits solidified Holtby as the number one goalie in Washington.

For the 6-foot-2, 203-pound Holtby, it was not a

but not before Holtby posted the best playoffs numbers of the season (for goaltending past the first round) with a .944 save percentage and 1.71 goals-against average.

In addition to Korn's coaching, the acquisition of two quality defensemen in the off-season also helped boost Holtby's game. Brooks Orpik and Matt Niskanen cost the Washington club a sizable amount of money, but these players were an investment with a great return. Overall, Trotz coached the team to be a better defensive club, but because Holtby played so many games in 2014–15, he also faced the most shots of any goalie (2,044). Luckily, he also made the most saves (1,887).

Going forward, the key for the 25-year-old Holtby

is to increase his playoff experience (he has played in 34 career postseason games but has a losing record of 16–18). This goes for the rest of the team as well. The Capitals are in a good position to be contenders for the Cup with players like Alex Ovechkin, Nicklas Backstrom, John Carlson and Marcus Johansson, but their playoff intensity needs to improve with more offense and timely scoring. If the Capitals do advance in the playoffs, there is no doubt that Holtby and his incredible postseason numbers will play a large role in that process.

CAREER HIGHLIGHTS

Drafted 93rd overall by the Washington Capitals in 2008

Leads all Washington Capitals goalies with a .921 save percentage

Led the NHL with 73 games played in 2014–15

Posted a 101–51–18 record in 178 career games

GOALTENDER

Henrik
LUNDQVIST
30

club couldn't beat the surging Kings that were peaking at just the right time. Determined to get his team back to the finals in 2015, Lundqvist returned from a serious neck injury and 25-game absence to lead the Rangers into the playoffs again (then-backup goalie Cam Talbot was a huge help in keeping the team alive during that time). He played well against the Pittsburgh Penguins in the first round, holding them at eight goals in five games. The Washington Captials were tougher to beat, but the Rangers came back from a 3–1 deficit to take the series in seven games. The Tampa Bay Lightning proved to be an entirely different challenge and there were times Lundqvist struggled badly against the Florida-based squad, allowing a total of 12 goals in back-to-back games. The teams ended up pushing themselves to seven games with the Lightning coming out victorious in a 2–0 win. This was Lundqvist's first-ever Game 7 loss on home ice and his record dropped to 6–2 when playing a seventh game.

Before the 2015 postseason began, the Rangers were in a great position to win the Cup. They had claimed the Presidents' Trophy for the best regular-season record with 53 wins and 113 points and had placed third in goals for and 28th in goals against. They also boasted a fantastic group of defensemen. A late-season deal with the Arizona Coyotes had added blue-liner Keith Yandle, who joined Marc Staal, Dan Girardi, Dan Boyle, Kevin Klein and team captain Ryan McDonagh. The Rangers won seven play-off games by a score of 2–1, which is indicative of how well Lundqvist played behind this quality group of defensemen, but the truth of the matter was that many of the blue-liners were playing through injuries. And, unfortunately, the forwards on the team simply couldn't score often enough in order to give the New York club any hope of winning against a young, fast team like the Lightning (the Rangers were held scoreless in two of the last three games versus Tampa Bay).

Despite the recent hardships Lundqvist has endured,

New York Rangers goaltender Henrik Lundqvist has accomplished just about everything possible over his 10 seasons in the NHL. He has made both the First and Second All-Star Teams (2011–12 and 2012–13, respectively), taken home the Vezina Trophy for best goaltender in 2012, won a gold medal at the Olympics for Sweden in 2006, placed in the top 10 among goalies for wins and goals-against average eight times, and placed in the top 10 for his save percentage seven times. There is only one thing Lundqvist still has to do and that is win the Stanley Cup.

The Rangers made it to the Stanley Cup final in 2014 for the first time since 1994, but were beaten by the Los Angeles Kings in five games. Lundqvist did his best throughout the 2014 postseason, but the New York

he is still one of the best goalies the NHL has ever seen. For active goalies, he is in fourth place for wins (339), third in goals-against average (2.26) and fourth in shutouts (55). He sits in third place for all-time leaders in save percentage (.921), just behind Dominik Hasek and Tuukka Rask. He has played in three All-Star games and has been nominated for the Vezina Trophy five times, the most of any Rangers goaltender. He is also the franchise leader in wins, save percentage and shutouts, but he still needs that Holy Grail in order to fully round out his career. Because of this obvious empty space on the trophy shelf, when the 2015 season was over for the Rangers, the New York press started comparing Lundqvist to another Big Apple athlete — Patrick Ewing. Ewing was one of the most dominant players in basketball during his era, but he never won an NBA championship. Hopefully, however, the 2015–16 season brings the New York Rangers the success the team needs to take "King Henrik" all the way.

CAREER HIGHLIGHTS

Drafted 205th overall by New York Rangers in 2000

Posted a 2.26 career goals-against average over 10 seasons

Recorded 55 career shutouts and a save percentage of .921

Posted a 339–208–65 record in 620 career games

GOALTENDER

Ryan
MILLER

30

Miller had posted an incredbile save percentage of .923 before his trade in 2014, and considering his team had a record of 17–34–8 at that point, Miller's mark was a real eye-opener. Things didn't click in St. Louis, however, and Miller's save percentage dropped to .903. The Blues' goaltending coach Corey Hirsch tried to make an alteration to Miller's approach by asking the new acquisition to play a little deeper in his net, but the 168-pound Miller was reluctant to change and the Midwest wasn't as welcoming as many had hoped.

The Blues still finished the 2013–14 regular season with 111 points before facing their division rivals, the Chicago Blackhawks, in the first round of the playoffs. The defending Stanley Cup champions were a tough test, and even though St. Louis pulled off back-to-back overtime wins to start the series, Chicago ousted the Blues in six games. The loss stung Miller, and with the problems he was having finding his game in St. Louis, he didn't re-sign with the team when the season was completed.

Meanwhile, the Vancouver Canucks were trying to escape the long shadows of goaltenders Roberto Luongo and Cory Schneider, so they tabbed Miller as the goalie of the future for their franchise. He brought veteran status and a stability in net that was badly needed inside the Vancouver crease.

After signing a three-year deal worth $18 million, things went well for Miller. He recorded his 300th career win on October 28, 2014, when Vancouver beat the Carolina Hurricanes 4–1, and when he overcame the Sabres 5–2 on January 30, 2015, Miller had officially registered a win against every NHL team. Soon afterward, however, Miller suffered a knee injury that limited his play to 45 games and the Canucks once again turned to Eddie Lack to bail them out of trouble. Lack turned in a fine performance, but without Miller playing first string in the playoffs, the Canucks were tossed from the first round by the surprising Calgary Flames.

Miller is a strong fundamentals goaltender who is

W hen goaltender Ryan Miller was traded from the Buffalo Sabres to the St. Louis Blues, it looked like a perfect match. The deal was completed on February 28, 2014, just as the Blues were getting into playoff mode. They paid a heavy price to complete the transaction (three players and two draft choices, including a first-rounder in 2015), but St. Louis didn't mind giving up a lot for the 6-foot-2 netminder — the team had visions of Miller taking the Blues all the way to the Stanley Cup final. Coach Ken Hitchcock emphasizes defense and that was going to be made even tighter with Miller in goal. But a funny thing happened on the way to the record books — the Blues never even came close to the final after being ousted in the first round of the playoffs.

rarely caught out of position. He spent many quality years toiling for Buffalo teams that didn't make the play-offs and the furthest he's been in the postseason is the Conference finals. He did lead the American Olympic team to within one goal of the gold medal in 2010, but he has yet to taste victory on any major stage. His numbers are impressive, regard-less: his career-high 41 wins and .929 save percentage won him the Vezina Trophy in 2009–10, he led the league in shots against and saves in 2012–13 and still holds first place in the Sabres' record books for most wins (284).

With two more years on his contract, Miller is in a prime position to have a statement season in 2015–16, espe-cially since Lack has been traded to the Carolina Hurricanes. Vancouver needs a big year from many of its players, but none more than Miller. The goaltend-ing situation has been a problem for the Canucks since they lost Game 7 of the 2011 Stanley Cup final, so a shutdown performance would go a long way toward fixing Vancouver's perceived crease conundrum. Such a performance would also help Miller shed his reputation as simply a great regular-season goaltender.

Drafted 138th overall by the Buffalo Sabres in 1999

Named to the First All-Star Team and awarded the Vezina Trophy in 2009–10

Has won 30 or more games seven times over 12 NHL seasons

Posted a 323–209–59 record in 604 career games

CAREER HIGHLIGHTS

GOALTENDER

Jonathan
QUICK

32

accomplished a lot in his short eight-year career.

One of the smaller goalies in the NHL today (listed at 6-foot-1 and 220 pounds), Quick was always in net, even while playing in road-hockey games growing up as a kid in Milford, Connecticut. He played high school hockey for the Avon Old Farms in his home state before attending the University of Massachusetts. The Kings liked what they saw after Quick went 19–12–5 in his second year with the university team, so they selected him in the third round of the 2005 draft. He became a professional in 2007–08 when he played for the Manchester Monarchs of the American Hockey League (AHL), where he had a save percentage of .921 after two seasons. By the 2008–09 campaign, Quick was with the Kings to stay, achieving 21 wins in 44 appearances as a rookie.

Quick gets so low to the ice that he looks smaller than his height indicates, but he relies on his lightning-fast reflexes to make up for any lack of size. His style allows him to see more pucks through traffic and his lateral movement is one of the best among all NHL goalies. Quick never gives up on a play and he uses his leg pads to great effectiveness when he slides across the ice to stop the puck. One of his most spectacular saves came in March 2011, when the Kings hosted the Calgary Flames. Jarome Iginla had the perfect shot on goal until Quick slid across the blue paint to make an incredible deflection. It kept the game scoreless and Los Angeles ended up winning 2–1.

Quick's terrific play has allowed him to post 35 or more wins four times in his career and make the playoffs five times. When the Kings won the Cup in 2012, he led all postseason goalies in save percentage (.946) and goals-against average (1.41), but when the Kings won the Cup again in 2014, Quick was not as dominant during the regular season or in the playoffs. Injuries held him to just to 49 starts in the regular season, but he still posted a respectable record of 27–17–4. The Kings

The Los Angeles Kings have been a part of the NHL since the 1967–68 season, but have never really had a great goaltender to rely on — that is, until Jonathan Quick arrived in the 2007–08 season. The Kings have had some success with netminders like Rogie Vachon and Kelly Hrudey (who actually took Los Angeles to the Stanley Cup final in 1993), but neither can match the performance of Quick, who is the only goalie to lead the team to not just one Stanley Cup, but two. He holds the franchise record for most career games played (407), wins (212), shutouts (37), goals-against average (2.27) and save percentage (.915). Quick was also the first member of the Los Angeles Kings to ever win the Conn Smythe Trophy (awarded to him as MVP of the 2012 playoffs). To put it simply, Quick has managed to sneak into the playoffs (finishing third in their division) and had to play seven games in the first three series. The first round against San Jose was the hardest because the Sharks were up 3–0 in games. The Kings carried on to win two more Game 7 match-ups on the road (over the Anaheim Ducks and Chicago Blackhawks) before taking the Cup on home ice in an overtime Game 5 against the New York Rangers. Quick was under tremendous pressure during each of his Game 7 situations, but he focused on getting the win and the result is obvious.

Quick has benefited from Kings coach Darryl Sutter's emphasis on defense, but the team failed to make the postseason in 2015.

Quick still won 36 games and managed to finish in the top 10 in wins, so if the Kings can work their way back to their former success, Quick and his teammates should have the chance to shine in the playoffs once again.

Drafted 72nd overall by the Los Angeles Kings in 2005

Led the league in shutouts in 2011–12 with 10

Holds fourth place in goals-against average for active goalies (2.27)

Winner of the William M. Jennings Trophy in 2013–14

Posted a 212–139–46 record in 407 career games

CAREER HIGHLIGHTS

Tuukka
RASK

GOALTENDER

40

Rask was worked into the Bruins' lineup slowly and methodically. He came to North America for the 2007–08 season and played on the Bruins' farm team in Providence, Rhode Island. Over two full years there, he posted a 60–33–6 record and was one of the best goalies in the American Hockey League (AHL). Boston then made Rask the NHL club's backup for the 2009–10 season, but he actually ended up splitting the games with his counterpart Tim Thomas due to Thomas' drop-off in wins. Rask finished with unbelievable numbers: a league-leading save percentage of .931 and goals-against average of 1.97, plus a 22–12–5 record. He also got his first postseason experience in net, but the Bruins couldn't get past the Philadelphia Flyers in the second round.

The following season saw Thomas return to his former glory and Rask got to watch as the Vezina winner battled his way to individual accolades and, ultimately, the 2011 Stanley Cup. The lockout-shortened year of 2012–13 saw the departure of Thomas and the crease was finally Rask's for the taking. He won 19 of his 34 starts in the 48-game regular schedule and played in all 22 Bruins games in the 2013 postseason. The Bruins' first-round series against the surprising Maple Leafs went right to Game 7, when Toronto infamously collapsed in the third period and Rask held on in overtime to allow his team to score and move on to the second round. Things got easier as the Bruins ousted the New York Rangers in five games and swept the Pittsburgh Penguins before losing the final to the Chicago Blackhawks in six hard-fought contests. Two of the Bruins' losses in the final were in overtime and one of those games saw Rask stop 59 of 63 shots as the first game of the series went into triple overtime (with the Blackhawks prevailing by a score of 4–3). Nevertheless, Rask had shown in a short amount of time that he was capable of taking a team all the way, and he had erased any doubt that he might not be a top goalie at the NHL level.

The Toronto Maple Leafs needed a goaltender of the future, and in 2005, with the 21st pick in the draft, they selected Tuukka Rask. As a highly regarded netminding prospect from Finland, Rask had turned heads at the World Juniors in 2006, leading Finland to a bronze medal while also being named to the tournament All-Star Team and earning praise as the best goaltender of the championships. But Toronto needed a more immediate stopgap, so Rask was traded to the Boston Bruins for Andrew Raycroft, a former rookie of the year.

Now Raycroft is retired and Rask is an undisputed All-Star as well as the 2014 Vezina Trophy winner as the best goaltender in the league. Regret might not be a big enough word for the Maple Leafs organization.

Buoyed by his playoff performance, Rask came back in the 2013–14 regular season to play in 58 games and record 36 wins. His excellent play throughout the year earned him the Vezina Trophy as well as a spot on the First All-Star Team. With a .930 save percentage and 2.04 goals-against average, it looked like the Bruins might go back to the Stanley Cup final once more, but their long-time nemesis, the Montreal Canadiens, upset them in the second round of the 2014 playoffs. Then, shockingly, in 2014–15, the Bruins missed the postseason altogether, even though Rask finished with a respectable 34 wins.

Rask is a good-sized goalie at 6-foot-2 and 185 pounds, and he is athletic with a touch of acrobatic flair. His glove hand is lightning-quick and his butterfly style allows him to take away the bottom of the net with ease. He is also now established as one of the best goalies in the entire league and Maple Leafs fans can only dream about what might have been had the 28-year-old stayed in Toronto.

Drafted 21st overall by the Toronto Maple Leafs in 2005

Recorded 26 career shutouts

Winner of the Vezina Trophy for the 2013–14 season

Has a career goals-against average of 2.17

Posted a 136–81–35 record in 266 career games

CAREER HIGHLIGHTS

Pekka
RINNE

GOALTENDER

35

its own. When Rinne was playing in his home country of Finland, one of the Predators' European scouts took a liking to him, even though he had only seen Rinne play in a couple of games. Then-assistant general manager Ray Shero went to Finland to see Rinne for himself, but could only watch the goalie in pre-game warmups because he wasn't slated to start. Still, it was enough to convince the Predators to draft him, though they made Rinne wait until the second-last round. Few teams have ever received such a return on a late selection like the Predators have with Rinne.

After three seasons with the Milwaukee Admirals of the American Hockey League (AHL), Rinne was called up to the NHL full-time in 2008–09. Two years later, Rinne broke out in the 2010–11 season. He finished second among goalies for save percentage (a career-high .930) and received his first Vezina Trophy nomination for best goaltender. He followed up in 2011–12 with a league-leading 43 wins, 73 games played and 1,987 saves. He also received another Vezina Trophy nomination, the first time a Nashville goaltender had ever received two in a row.

During the 2013–14 season, Rinne was limited to 24 games to close out a disaster season for his Nashville team that didn't even make the playoffs. He injured his hip and needed surgery only nine games into the season, but luckily he came back from his injury feeling strong — he suited up for eight games at the 2014 World Championships, taking his Finnish team all the way to the championship game. Despite losing to Russia, Rinne was named the most valuable player in the tournament.

After the washout of 2013–14, Nashville made the dramatic move of firing the only coach the franchise had ever known in Barry Trotz. Out was Trotz's defensive-minded system and in was Peter Laviolette, an offensive coach who most recently had taken the Philadelphia Flyers to the Stanley Cup final in 2010.

Rinne and the club responded well to the leadership

O f all the positions in hockey, goaltending has evolved the most. The majority of modern goalies are large athletes, strong skaters and deft puck-handlers. Of the current stars, few are as good as the Nashville Predators' Pekka Rinne, who, at 6-foot-5 and 204 pounds, is a prototype for a franchise netminder. He is an incredible combination of size and athleticism, and while he mostly uses the butterfly style of play, he also is smart enough to play standing up because he can take up so much of the net. Rinne is quick with his glove, is not afraid to leave his crease to play the puck and, along with his lightning-quick reflexes, has all the attributes NHL teams are now looking for in a netminder.

The fact that Rinne is in the NHL at all is a story of

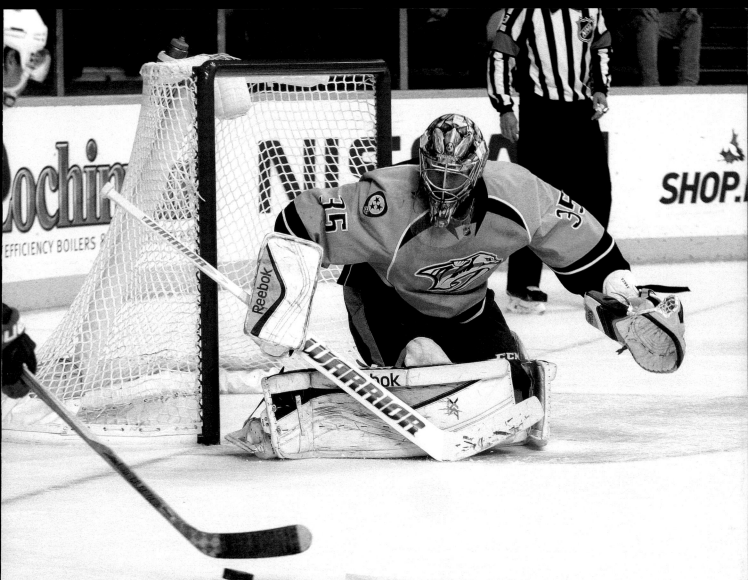

change, and the goaltender posted one of his best seasons in 2014–15. He finished in the top 10 in wins, save percentage and goals-against average (earning a third Vezina nomination), and Nashville racked up 104 points to easily return to the postseason.

The Predators were no match for the eventual Stanley Cup–winning Chicago Blackhawks, however, and in the first round of the 2015 playoffs were out of the running in six games. Of Rinne's four playoff appearances, he has only advanced to the second round on two occasions and his postseason record is a rather weak 15–19, but it is the only real blemish on a stellar seven-year career to date.

The native of Kempele, Finland, came to North America when he was 23 years old and with his savvy play and winning attitude has impressed management,

players and fans ever since.

The task now is to lead Nashville to the third round of the playoffs and beyond because setting franchise records is nice, but competing for the Stanely Cup is what every player truly wishes for.

Drafted 258th overall by the Nashville Predators in 2004

Franchise leader in wins, goals-against average, save percentage and shutouts

Finished in the top three in Vezina Trophy voting three times

Posted a 204–115–43 record in 381 career games

CAREER HIGHLIGHTS

DANGEROUS D-MEN

P.K.
SUBB

Tyler
MYERS

DEFENSE
57

Alex
PIETRANGELO   27

DEFENSE

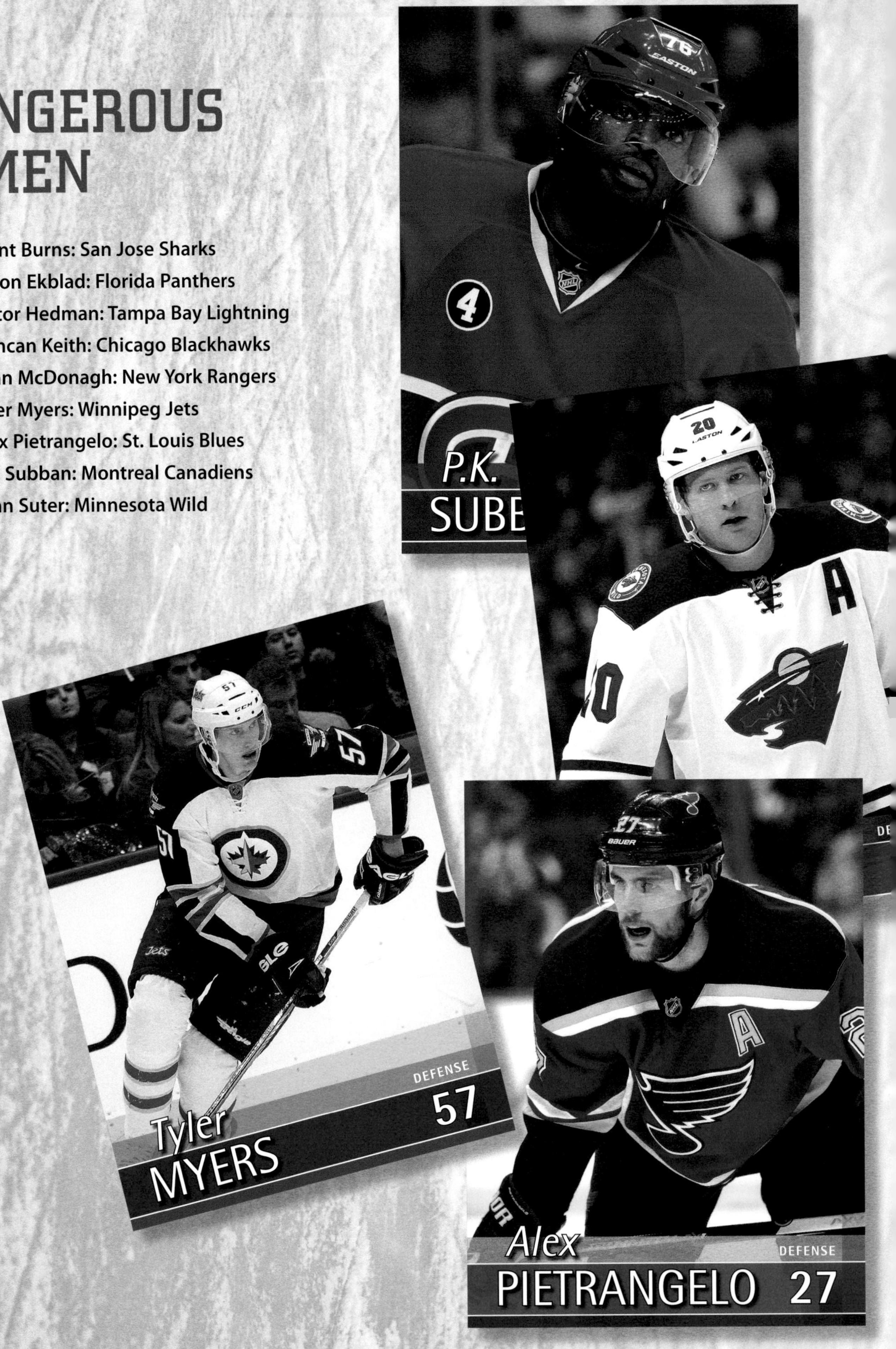

DEFENSE

Brent BURNS

88

When Peter DeBoer was named head coach of the San Jose Sharks on May 28, 2015, he was happy to be back behind a bench in the NHL for one of the most talented teams in the league. The Sharks' forward attack features high-end talent from the likes of Logan Couture, Joe Pavelski, Joe Thornton and Tommy Wingels. The defense is anchored by Marc-Edouard Vlasic, an Olympic gold medalist for Canada in 2014, along with some youngsters like Mirco Mueller and Brenden Dillon, who are starting to play a larger role on the blue line. What really must have put a smile on DeBoer's face, however, is that 6-foot-5, 230-pound Brent Burns is emerging as one of the better defensemen in the NHL after initially being drafted into the league as a forward.

DeBoer was an assistant coach with Team Canada at the 2015 World Championships and witnessed a great performance by Burns, who was named the best defenseman in the tournament. He scored two goals (one a game-winner), added nine assists and was a plus-12 in Canada's undefeated romp to win the gold medal. The big blue-liner was able to play for Canada because the Sharks missed the playoffs for the first time since 2002–03, but despite his team's poor season, Burns had his best ever with 60 points.

As first impressions go, Burns doesn't appear to be the typical NHL player. His arms are heavily tattooed, paying homage to his family members who served in the Canadian military; his home is nicknamed the "Burns Zoo" because of his collection of dogs, cats and snakes. He has long hair, a scruffy beard and is noticeably missing two front teeth. His attention-grabbing, multi-colored suits worn along with a camouflage backpack are also part of his look. Former Sharks coach Todd McLellan once called Burns "a free spirit" and it is definitely hard to argue with that.

But, Burns is also a very passionate and driven player, and when he is on his game, few opponents can handle him. In addition to being large, Burns is fast, physical and strong. He can shoot the puck with authority and can move it up the ice with a great pass. Burns' skill is further evident in the fact that he can play effectively as either a forward or defenseman — something that is now very rare in the NHL. Burns put up a 40-point season playing forward for his junior team, the Brampton Battalion, and with San Jose was moved to the right wing for a good portion of the 2013–14 season, popping in 22 goals for the Sharks while playing alongside Thornton, the best center on the team. He could have stayed up front, but when the San Jose team decided not to bring back defenseman Dan Boyle, it was Burns who was moved back to the blue line for the 2014–15 campaign. Naturally, it took some time for

Burns to adjust to playing defense again, but overall he didn't mind the shift to what many opine is his natural position. He led the Sharks' defense in points, shots on goal, penalty minutes and time on ice — each statistic clear evidence that he is useful at both ends of the rink. Burns only has a plus-4 rating over his entire 11-season career, meaning DeBoer will certainly want him to work on that since he likes to emphasize a defense-first style of playing.

San Jose struck a significant deal to acquire Burns from the Minnesota Wild (the team that drafted him in 2003), giving up a first-round draft choice and two players (including defenseman Charlie Coyle), and the Sharks still see more good things on the horizon for Burns if he can stay healthy and focused. He is a family

man now and as a result, the 30-year-old might move toward being a little less eccentric off the ice and more dominating on it.

Drafted 20th overall by the Minnesota Wild in 2003

Recorded five NHL seasons with double-digit goal totals

Won the 2015 NHL Foundation Player Award for enriching his community

Recorded 114 goals and 348 points in 715 career games

CAREER HIGHLIGHTS

Aaron EKBLAD

DEFENSE 5

In 2014, the Florida Panthers had the first overall pick for the second time in team history. General manager Dale Tallon, who had plenty of experience building teams with a youthful core, saw this as an opportunity to gain a quality player the Panthers could develop. Tallon had previously overseen the drafting of Jonathan Toews and Patrick Kane during his time as general manager with the Chicago Blackhawks, and this appeared to be proof that Tallon's methods worked. So, when draft day arrived, Tallon selected defenseman Aaron Ekblad at No. 1, much like the Florida club had done with blue-liner Ed Jovanovski back in 1994. Jovanovski was prominent when the Panthers made it to the Stanley Cup final in 1996, and if Ekblad's rookie year was any indication, the Panthers looked like they

had selected another defenseman who could not only take the team to the playoffs, but also help them win the championship.

When Ekblad reported for training camp in September 2014, the 18-year-old appeared nervous and unsure. His performance during the preseason was nothing special, but the 6-foot-4, 216-pound native of Belle River, Ontario, had nothing left to prove in the juniors (he had 53 points in 58 games for the Barrie Colts in 2013–14), so the Panthers kept him on their roster to start the year. As soon as the regular season began, Ekblad gained some confidence and began to get into a groove.

He had a total of 39 points in 81 games and displayed maturity well beyond his years. At one point Ekblad was averaging over 22 minutes a game before ending up at 21:49 for the season. Ekblad's play helped the Panthers reach 91 points (the team's best result since the 2011–12 season) and challenge for a playoff spot, of which the Panthers came up just seven points short. Playing defense in the NHL at such a young age (Ekblad turned 19 in February 2015) is a difficult assignment, but this player had proved it could be done — and done well.

Not only is Ekblad a talented player, he is fortunate enough to be surrounded by an incredible support system. He was paired with veteran defenseman Brian Campbell, and his steadying influence on the rookie helped Ekblad improve his game immensely. He also lived with Panthers captain Willie Mitchell and his family, which gave Ekblad much needed off-ice stability. But the most advantageous influence in Ekblad's life came from his agent and mentor, the legendary Bobby Orr. Ekblad's relationship with Orr began when he was just 13 years old. His father David had decided Orr was going to be Ekblad's agent, and so he arranged a meeting with the former Boston Bruins star. It has been noted how Ekblad uses these resources to help make him a better player. All of these supportive examples around Ekblad have won Stanley Cups and they cannot

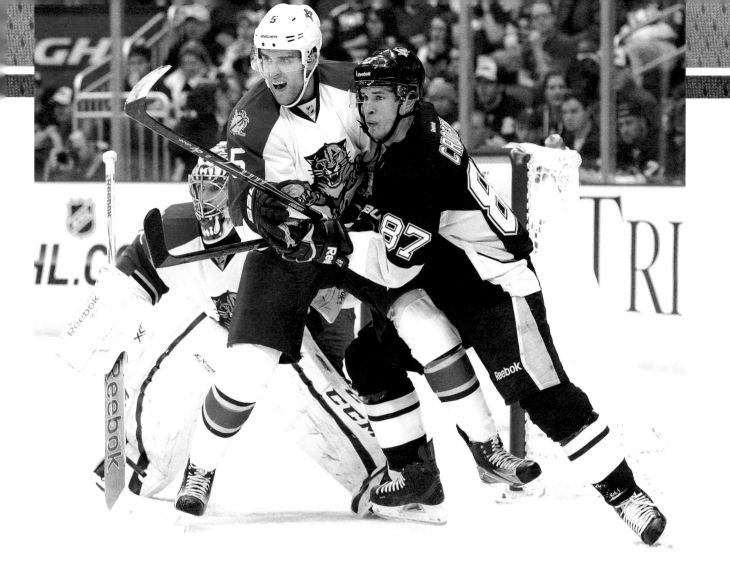

help but influence the polite and well-mannered Ekblad in all the right ways.

One of Ekblad's main attributes is his ability to work the power play. He displays poise running the point with the extra man and his accurate shot earned him six goals with the man advantage. Ekblad is a smart player and usually makes the right choices, so the more NHL experience he gets, the more he will be able to hone his natural abilities. His skating may not be at the elite level, but he is rarely caught out of position and he makes a determined effort to skate hard to get back to his own end. Ekblad is an impressive plus-12 as a first-year player and has four game-winning goals, the most of any rookie defenseman in 2014–15. His skills clearly indicate that he knows how to play the game at both ends of the ice, which is why he won the Calder Memorial Trophy in 2015 for best rookie.

There are many key young players on the Panthers team, including previous Calder winner Jonathan Huberdeau. Others, such as Nick Bjugstad, Erik Gudbranson, Jimmy Hayes and Dmitri Kulikov, are also important aspects of the Panthers' rebuild. None, however, may be as crucial as Ekblad, who could easily be a franchise defenseman.

Drafted 1st overall by the Florida Panthers in 2014

Played in the 2015 NHL All-Star Game

Won the Calder Trophy as best rookie for 2014–15

Recorded 12 goals and 39 points in 81 career games

CAREER HIGHLIGHTS

Victor
HEDMAN
DEFENSE
77

The Tampa Bay Lightning selected 6-foot-6 defenseman Victor Hedman second overall in the 2009 entry draft with the expectation that they could count on the young blue-liner to anchor their defense for years to come. It took Hedman a few seasons to make an impact, and throughout his first few years playing professionally, he didn't give a lot of indication that he was going to be anything extraordinary. Hedman's performance during the 2013–14 season changed all that as a 55-point campaign suddenly put his name in the discussion about who was the best defenseman in the league. He followed this up with another good year in 2014–15 that also included a great playoff run.

Hedman hails from Ornskoldsvik, Sweden, an area in

Europe that has produced many NHL players, including Peter Forsberg, Markus Naslund and the Sedin twins, Henrik and Daniel. Hedman grew up idolizing these athletes, but he never thought overly hard about making hockey his career. He skated for fun on a small outdoor rink close to his home and he used to put on goalie pads so that his brothers could practice their shots on him. Eventually his father Olle got involved and told him that he could get a new helmet if he would play anywhere else but in net, so Hedman made the shift to defense and never looked back.

Hedman was tall and skinny growing up, which made him a bit uncoordinated, but as he advanced in the Swedish minor hockey system, the NHL scouts started to notice his skills. He played with the Modo Hockey organization right up until he was drafted, when he came to North America for the first time. Tampa Bay decided to thrust him into their lineup right away as an 18-year-old, which meant there was no time for him to develop in the minors.

He had a respectable rookie year in which he recorded 20 points (good for seventh place among rookie defensemen that season), but Hedman got his first taste of real NHL success when the Lightning made it to the Eastern Conference final during his sophomore season in 2011. Unfortunately, they ended up losing to the Boston Bruins in seven games, which began a two-year slump for the Tampa Bay club.

In 2013–14, Jon Cooper took over as head coach of the Lightning, and this is when Hedman also enjoyed a notable year. He led his team in assists and led all Lightning defensemen in goals, points and average time on ice. Tampa Bay also made it back into the playoffs, but were swept by the Montreal Canadiens.

The 2015 postseason was even more incredible for Hedman, as his team got past the Detroit Red Wings, Montreal Canadiens and New York Rangers to reach the Stanley Cup final where the Lightning faced off

against the Chicago Blackhawks. Tampa Bay won two of the first three games to start the final and Hedman was prominent in establishing the lead for his team. During the third game of the series, hockey fans saw the best of Hedman as he set up two goals in a 3–2 Lightning victory. He had an end-to-end pass to Ryan Callahan and a long rush to set up Cedric Paquette with the game winner. Hedman was now attacking and defending with equal effectiveness, as he finished the playoffs with 14 points in 26 games and had the second-best rating of plus-11.

Hedman has matured alongside his team, and his defensive partner, Anton Stralman, has made for the perfect pairing, since both players are great skaters and puckhandlers. Up front, the Lightning are a dynamic team, which means that Hedman has plenty of targets to hit with his superior passing skills. The 2015 playoffs also provided a glimpse of what the Tampa Bay club might be able to achieve in the future now that the hockey world is aware they have a gem on defense who can lead the team to greater heights.

Drafted 2nd overall by the Tampa Bay Lightning in 2009

Holds 10th place on the Lightning's all-time list for assists (143)

Finished second in points with 14 for all defensemen in the 2015 playoffs

Recorded 39 goals and 182 points in 392 career games

CAREER HIGHLIGHTS

Duncan KEITH

DEFENSE

2

The sixth game of the 2015 Stanley Cup final was tied at 0–0 late in the second period with the hometown Chicago Blackhawks in position to win their third championship in six years. The Blackhawks were battling the Tampa Bay Lightning and both teams were working hard to score first, as they had both gone 11–1 in the playoffs when getting the puck in the net before the opposition. Suddenly, the Blackhawks caught a break when winger Patrick Kane took a long pass inside the Lightning zone and cleverly waited for Duncan Keith to catch up. Kane fed the hard-charging defenseman the puck and Keith put a shot right on goal. Lightning netminder Ben Bishop made the save but Keith followed up with the rebound that was waiting for him. He corralled the puck and deposited a shot

into the net for the opening goal of the game with just 2:47 to go in the second period. Keith's effort was the championship-winning tally and it helped him clinch the Conn Smythe Trophy as the best performer in the playoffs. It was a perfect ending for Keith who had a memorable postseason, earning the right to have his name engraved on the Stanley Cup for the third time.

To fully understand the enormity of Keith's performance in the 2015 playoffs, it's important to consider a couple of vital statistics. Firstly, Keith played more than 700 minutes across 23 postseason games. He also played in 80 regular-season games and led his fellow blue-liners in average time on ice (25:34). The Blackhawks had relied heavily on him because of injured teammates and coach Joel Quenneville's reluctance to use his fifth and sixth defensemen to any great degree.

Secondly, Keith is not only a durable player, but he also has a clutch shot. He had three goals in the 2015 playoffs, all of which were game-winners. Thirdly and finally, Keith is tied in fifth for playoff assists by a defenseman in a single-season, with 18. The only blue-liners who recorded more were Paul Coffey (25), Al MacInnis (24), Brian Leetch (23) and Bobby Orr (19) — all of whom are in the Hall of Fame, which is where Keith is undoubtedly headed as soon as his career is over.

When Chicago drafted the 6-foot-1, 200-pound Keith 54th overall in 2002, they looked at the blue-liner as a long-term project. He had produced a lot of success in the minor leagues (118 points in 119 games for the Penticton Panthers of the British Columbia Hockey League), but had a long way to go before becoming a top-tier NHL defenseman. His dedication to the game and commitment to improving served him well. He spent two seasons with the Norfolk Admirals of the American Hockey League (AHL) before moving up to the Blackhawks for the 2005–06 season.

Since his entry into the NHL 10 years ago, Keith

CAREER HIGHLIGHTS

has won just about everything there is to win. He has two gold medals with Team Canada, two James Norris Memorial trophies as the league's best defenseman and two First All-Star Team honors. Keith could sit back and enjoy his achievements, but he is a driven player who keeps trying to win until he can't play anymore. The versatile blue-liner is blessed with a tremendous capacity to play for a long time and not get tired. It's not inconceivable that he could play an entire game if he had to (his fitness level is known to be off the charts). Keith's stamina is an inspiration to everyone on the Chicago team and they seem to feed off his energy, which was clearly the case throughout the 2015 playoff grind.

There is no doubt that Keith has benefited greatly from playing alongside Brent Seabrook and Niklas Hjalmarsson, who have also patrolled the Chicago blue line for three Stanley Cups. Simply put, Keith is one of the most valuable players on the Blackhawks' roster and one of the best defensemen the NHL has ever seen.

Ryan
McDONAGH

DEFENSE

27

McDonagh was born in St. Paul, Minnesota, one of the most hockey-oriented cities in the United States. He went to Cretin-Derham Hall High School and as a junior led his team to its first-ever state hockey championship. During his senior season, McDonagh received the 2007 Minnesota Mr. Hockey award, given annually to the top graduating high school player in the state. That same year, he won a silver medal playing for the United States at the IIHF World U-18 Championships. It didn't take long for NHL scouts to take notice of the smooth-skating defender and the Canadiens took him in the first round of the 2007 draft. Following the trading of his rights to New York, McDonagh decided to leave the University of Wisconsin after three successful years (46 points in 119 games) and signed an entry-level contract with the Rangers in July 2010. He started off with the team's American Hockey League (AHL) affiliate, the Connecticut Whale, but the big team called him up in January 2011 to join former Wisconsin teammate Derek Stepan in the New York lineup.

It looked like the 6-foot-1, 213-pound McDonagh was going to be a strong blue-liner who stuck with his superb defensive skills, but by the end of his second season, he had seven goals and 32 points on the year, indicating he was going to have some offensive flair, just like he did in high school and in college. He had his best offensive season in 2013–14 when he recorded 14 goals and 43 points. McDonagh thrived under coach Alain Vigneault and the Rangers not only made the playoffs but went all the way to the Stanley Cup final for the first time since 1994. McDonagh scored 17 points in the postseason (good for second among defensemen on his team) and was one of New York's best players, even though they fell to the Los Angeles Kings in five games.

McDonagh's excellent all-round play earned him the Rangers' captaincy prior to the start of the 2014–15 regular season and he is now working under a six-year

Bob Gainey was one of the best NHL players when he patrolled the left wing for the Montreal Canadiens during his 16-year career that included five Stanley Cups. He then became a top coach and executive for the Dallas Stars (winning another Cup as the team's general manager) before returning to Montreal to run the Habs' front office in 2003. It was here that Gainey made an error that would remain one of his few regrets. Gainey acquired winger Scott Gomez in exchange for the rights to Ryan McDonagh, a player the Canadiens had drafted 12th overall in 2007. Gomez made little of his time as a Hab and is now long gone from Montreal, while McDonagh is one of the best defensemen in the NHL. Mistakes like that can haunt a general manager for years.

contract worth $28.2 million that he signed in 2013. His teammates admire his leadership skills, as he is honest when speaking to the media and remains calm in the face of adversity.

The Rangers had a great season in 2014–15, clinching the Presidents' Trophy for finishing first in the league in points with 113, and many hockey pundits had the team pegged to win the Cup. That dream, however, was squashed by the Tampa Bay Lightning, who took the Rangers out of the Eastern Conference final in seven games. McDonagh played with a foot injury and it was clear he was not himself against the Lightning, finishing with a minus-2 rating in the third round.

The Rangers need more scoring and balance if they are to reach their goal of winning the Cup, but that will not be easy in the salary-cap era. That means McDonagh and the other defensemen will have to chip in on the attack if the New York Rangers are to capture their glory years in the seasons to come.

Drafted 12th overall by the Montreal Canadiens in 2007

Led all Rangers in shorthanded goals in 2013–14, with three

Recorded 25 or more assists three times

Recorded 34 goals and 136 points in 317 career games

CAREER HIGHLIGHTS

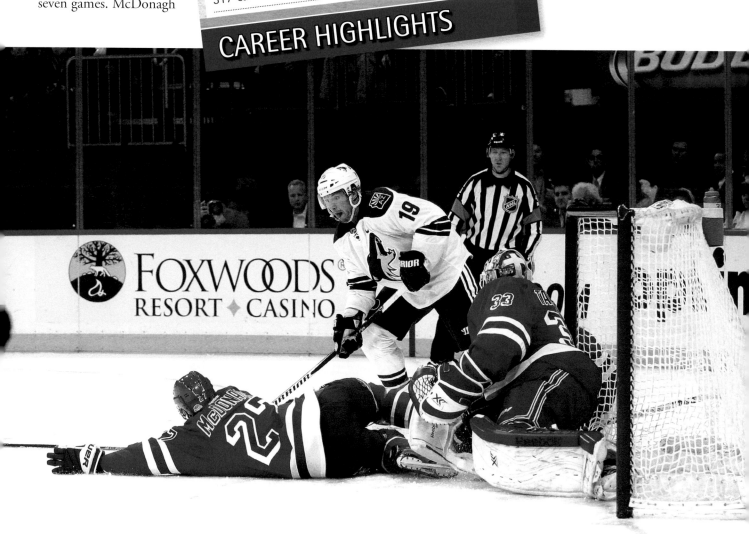

Tyler
MYERS

DEFENSE
57

to have his players establish themselves as a large, physical team that played a robust game on a nightly basis. Myers' physical dimensions made him a perfect fit for the Jets' blue line — his long reach forces skaters wide to the boards where their offensive forays can be snuffed out. And while he isn't a bruiser (averaging only about 45 penalty minutes a season), his tremendous size allows him to fit right in with the Winnipeg style.

Myers responded well to the trade, posting 15 points in just 24 games for the Jets while playing an average of just under 24 minutes a night. Perhaps more impressive, however, is that his plus/minus underwent more than a 20-point swing, going from a minus-15 rating in 47 games in Buffalo to a plus-9 rating by the end of the season. The Jets were thrilled with the big blue-liner's resurgence, and his addition helped the team grind out a playoff berth, holding off the defending champion Los Angeles Kings and perennial favorite San Jose Sharks toward the end of the season.

Myers came to be a hockey player in a somewhat unconventional manner. He was born in Houston, Texas, but moved to Calgary, Alberta, at 10 years of age when his father was transferred there because of his job in the oil industry. Had Myers stayed in Texas, it is almost certain — given his athletic gifts and size — he would have been groomed for the baseball diamond or football field. But in Canada, hockey was his calling, and by the age of 15 he was playing at the famous Athol Murray College of Notre Dame high school in Saskatchewan. He then played four years for the Kelowna Rockets, where he registered 77 points in 191 games before jumping to the Sabres.

Selected 12th overall in 2008, Myers had an outstanding rookie season as a 19-year-old. He played in all 82 games, scored 11 goals and added 37 assists while skating for a team-leading 23:44 per game — monster totals for a rookie defenseman. He even had a two-goal night in January 2010 against the Toronto Maple Leafs,

I t isn't every day that a 6-foot-8, 220-pound defenseman with offensive upside and shutdown skills is available on the trade market, but such was the case at the 2014–15 trade deadline. The flatlining Buffalo Sabres decided to move Tyler Myers, their blue-chip defenseman, to the Winnipeg Jets in exchange for the oft-troubled sniper, Evander Kane. The swap came as a relief for Myers because the Sabres were embarking on a years-long rebuild, and while players will seldom publically admit to wanting out of teardown situations, the move to a playoff contender was certainly a welcome change.

The Jets, barely four years into their relocation to Winnipeg, had forged a new identity under coach Paul Maurice in the 2014–15 campaign. Maurice worked

including the game-winning shot. His fine play through-out the season earned him the Calder Memorial Trophy as the best rookie over Jimmy Howard, Matt Duchene and John Tavares.

Six seasons into his big-league career, Myers looks to be on a similar track to another rangy, offensively gifted defenseman — Victor Hedman — who, like Myers, also needed some seasoning and a winning atmosphere around him in order to truly break through. The 2015 postseason was the first time the Jets made the playoffs since 2006–07 (when they were the Atlanta Thrashers), and in the first-round series against the Anaheim Ducks, Myers led all Jets players in time on ice. The playoffs didn't last long, though, as Winnipeg was swept by the equally large and rough Anaheim. Going forward, the strong starts and late-period collapses are points the team will address, and it is certain that the defensive core — including Myers — will be called on to tighten up in the final moments of games.

In addition to Myers, young guns such as Jacob Trouba, Josh Morrissey, Ben Chiarot, Mark Scheifele, Adam Lowry and Brendan Lemieux are all either up-and-coming or firmly on the roster, which makes Winnipeg's future look like an exciting one for players and fans alike.

Drafted 12th overall by the Buffalo Sabres in 2008

Winner of the Calder Memorial Trophy in 2010

Part of the 2009–10 First All-Rookie Team

Recorded 48 goals and 166 points in 389 career games

CAREER HIGHLIGHTS

DEFENSE

Alex
PIETRANGELO 27

When the 2012–13 season ended, the St. Louis Blues were determined to do whatever it took to re-sign defenseman Alex Pietrangelo. The Blues' general manager Doug Armstrong saw Pietrangelo as an elite defender and wanted to lock him into a long-term deal. By the end of the negotiations, the St. Louis club had given the 6-foot-3, 201-pound blue-liner a seven-year contract worth $45 million. Considering Pietrangelo is sixth on the franchise's list of all-time defensemen for career points (218) and fourth for game-winning goals (10), both parties are likely pretty happy with the deal.

The Blues have built a large part of their team around Pietrangelo and other quality blue-liners like Kevin Shattenkirk and Jay Bouwmeester. The team allowed

just 201 goals against in 2014–15, the fourth-best mark in the NHL, which helped the team win 51 games, record 109 points and take first place in the Central Division. The 2015 postseason, however, was a different story. The Blues were once again ousted from the playoffs in the first round, this time by the wild-card Minnesota Wild. It marked the fourth consecutive season the Blues went home early despite a great season under coach Ken Hitchcock. Many hockey experts blame disjointed goaltending by Brian Elliot and Jake Allen, but everyone needs to take their share of the disappointment, including Pietrangelo, who only had two assists in six games.

Outside of the playoffs, the St. Louis club can't complain about Pietrangelo, who they selected in the 2008 entry draft. There were many quality defensemen available that year — such as Luke Schenn, Tyler Myers and Erik Karlsson — but when it came time for the Blues to select, they picked the King City, Ontario, native Pietrangelo fourth overall (third defenseman chosen behind Drew Doughty and Zach Bogosian). Prior to being selected, Pietrangelo put up 44 points in 44 games playing for the Toronto Jr. Canadiens of the Greater Toronto Hockey League (GTHL) and racked up a further 52 points in 59 games for the Mississauga IceDogs of the Ontario Hockey League (OHL). The Blues wisely sent Pietrangelo back to the OHL to hone his skills, and they let him stay there until he was 20 years old. His first full season as a member of the Blues didn't come until 2010–11 when he produced 43 points in 79 games (the best of any Blues defenseman that season). The following campaign saw Pietrangelo notch 12 goals and 51 points in 81 games. He also earned his first Second All-Star Team honors and proved that the Blues organization made the right choice in selecting him.

Pietrangelo is a durable player for someone who plays as much as he does (he has led his team in average time on ice for four consecutive seasons) and has only missed seven games since his debut campaign in 2010–11. When fellow blue-liner Shattenkirk was badly injured in February 2015, Pietrangelo picked up the slack and posted 46 points, good for 14th place among all NHL defensemen that season. He is not an aggressive player (he tops out at 36 penalty minutes in 2011–12), but he shows superior skills when handling the puck. Pietrangelo is one the best passers among NHL defenseman and this gives him plenty of time on the power play (he has registered 76 career power-play points to date). His skills were utilized at the 2014 Winter

CAREER HIGHLIGHTS

Olympics when he partnered with Bouwmeester as a shutdown pair that allowed Team Canada to go undefeated in the tournament.

By this point Pietrangelo has established himself as one of the best all-round defensemen, which explains why he has twice been in the top 5 for James Norris Memorial Trophy contention. Judging by his career thus far, he has a good chance of claiming the trophy in the future, as at just 25 years old, Pietrangelo has accomplished a lot for the St. Louis Blues and will hopefully continue to do so in the years to come.

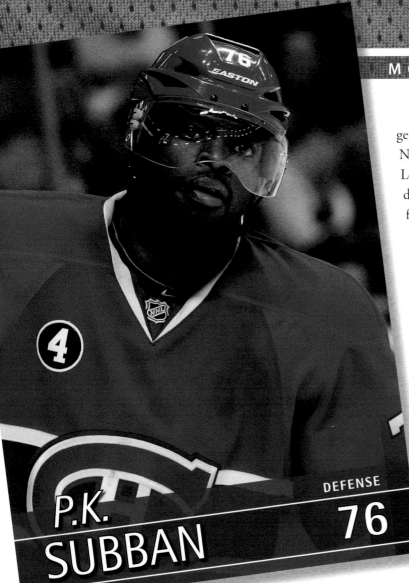

P.K.
SUBBAN

DEFENSE
76

get hit, but when the native of Toronto joined the North York Canadiens of the Greater Toronto Hockey League (GTHL), the coach decided to move him to defense because his skating was not up to par for a forward. Bigger and bulkier than most of boys he played against, Subban quickly became an effective defenseman. At the age of 15, he played for the GTHL's Markham Islanders (posting 43 points in 67 games) and then made the Belleville Bulls of the Ontario Hockey League (OHL). He was a solid player for the Bulls, collecting 190 points over four seasons, but NHL scouts were more excited about other defensemen and Subban hung around the OHL until the second round of the 2007 draft before being taken by the Montreal Canadiens as the 43rd overall choice.

After one year of playing with Montreal's affiliate in the American Hockey League (AHL), Subban joined the Canadiens as a 21-year-old in 2010–11 and quickly left an impression on the league. He scored 14 goals, a tremendous total for a rookie defenseman, but he also rubbed many opponents the wrong way with his cocky nature and lack of respect. As a result, he piled up 124 minutes in penalties in his first NHL season and 119 more in his second. The Habs were not quite sure what they were up against, but they signed the 6-foot, 217-pound Subban to a two-year extension so they could get a better read on the brash defender. When he was awarded the James Norris Memorial Trophy in 2013, Montreal knew they had one of the NHL's more impactful defensemen. He was the sixth Canadiens blue-liner to win the trophy, as he had just put out 38 points in 42 games in the lockout-shortened season of 2012–13. The other five Montreal winners — Doug Harvey, Tom Johnson, Jacques Lapperiere, Larry Robinson and Chris Chelios — are all members of the Hockey Hall of Fame. Subban may have enough drive and ambition to pull off joining that elite group one day.

Subban had his most productive year to date in

Pernell Karl "P.K." Subban is one of the most popular players on the Montreal Canadiens team and his enthusiasm is infectious. The Bell Centre crowd reacts well to Subban's passion (while opposing team's fans boo him with equal fervor), and he has proven his eight-year, $72-million deal — the richest ever given out by the Montreal franchise — is well deserved for the Canadiens' leading defenseman in points for the last five seasons.

Subban wasn't a defenseman when he first started playing hockey. At 10 years old, he could shoot a puck better than most other kids and was able to use his blazing drive more effectively at the center position. Opponents were so intimidated by Subban's powerful shot that they would get out of the way so as to not

2014–15 with several career-high statistics, including 15 goals, 60 points, a plus-21 rating and 5 game-winning goals. And while the Habs finished second overall in the regular season with 110 points, they had a disappointing playoff run when the Tampa Bay Lightning ended their year after six games in the semifinals.

Subban can hit like a sledgehammer and he makes opposing forwards pay a physical price when forechecking; he also loves to level hip-checks on speedy wingers trying to beat him to the outside. On the offensive side of the game, Subban possesses a wicked shot and the Canadiens rely on his blistering slapper to find the back of the net. Subban, however, seems to sometimes play by his own rules and is unafraid of making mistakes. That mindset can lead to odd-man rushes or having to take a penalty to get back into the play and thwart

a scoring chance, but his gambling can also pay off with excellent playmaking and highlight-reel goals.

Regardless of criticism, what Montreal lacks is exactly what Subban brings to the team — scoring and size. If the Canadiens can add a few more players that share his talents, the Habs will be a force to be reckoned with.

Drafted 43rd overall by the Montreal Canadiens in 2007

Named to the First All-Star Team in 2013 and 2015

Has 38 points in 55 playoff games

Recorded 57 goals and 227 points in 366 career games

CAREER HIGHLIGHTS

Ryan
SUTER

DEFENSE

20

year came in 2002–03 when he had 24 points in 42 games before being selected seventh overall by the Nashville Predators at the 2003 entry draft. Suter didn't jump directly into the NHL and played one year at the University of Wisconsin before going to the American Hockey League (AHL) to start his pro career with the Milwaukee Admirals in the 2004–05 season (scoring 23 points in 63 games). He then joined the Predators for the 2005–06 campaign, scoring one goal and adding 15 assists. Suter played seven strong seasons for the Nashville club, making the playoffs in six of those years. During these seasons, the Predators advanced past the first round on two occasions but were never able to go any further (Suter only had 13 points in 39 postseason games). By the end of the 2011–12 season Suter was an unrestricted free agent, despite the Predators' best efforts to re-sign him.

The Minnesota Wild pursued Suter relentlessly. Wild general manager Chuck Fletcher ended up pulling off a major coup by signing both Suter and New Jersey Devils star Zach Parise with matching $98-million contracts that are spread over 13 years. Both players were 27 years old at the time but the team felt they were worthwhile investments. In reality, neither player is likely to be with the Wild until they are 40, but both have characteristics — grit and consistency — that make Minnesota a tough team to beat.

Suter made it clear that his main motivation for signing with the Wild was not his large contract but the fact that he could play closer to his family. Suter's first year in Minnesota was the lockout-shortened season of 2012–13, but he still had a good 48-game campaign. He led all Minnesota defensemen in assists (28), average time on ice (27:17) and power-play points (15). He was also named to the NHL's First All-Star Team after recording 32 points, and was the runner-up to the Montreal Canadiens' P.K. Subban in the voting for the James Norris Memorial Trophy as the league's best

Minnesota Wild defenseman Ryan Suter is part of one of the greatest North American hockey families. His uncle Gary was a star defenseman for the Calgary Flames and won the Stanley Cup with them in 1989. Bob Suter, Ryan's father, was a defenseman on the famous 1980 U.S. Olympic team that won a gold medal at Lake Placid. With this background, it's no wonder that Ryan was smitten with hockey at an early age and, more than anything else, dreamed of winning a gold medal at the Winter Olympics, just like his father.

Inspired by his family's hockey achievements, the native of Madison, Wisconsin, played high school hockey and was 17 years old when he joined the USA Hockey National Team Development Program. His best

defenseman. His personal success also helped his team get back to the postseason for the first time in five years.

Suter had his best season in 2013–14 when he recorded a career-high 43 points and 29:25 average time on ice. The Wild returned to the playoffs in which Suter contributed seven points, but the team lost to the Chicago Blackhawks in six games. The following season got off to a terrible start for Suter because his father suddenly passed away at the age of 57. The Wild also struggled early on in the season, sitting in last place in the Central Division, but halfway through the campaign, Minnesota acquired goaltender Devan Dubnyk from the Arizona Coyotes

CAREER HIGHLIGHTS

Drafted 7th overall by the Nashville Predators in 2003

Won silver with Team USA at the 2010 Winter Olympics

Ranks fifth in franchise history for Wild defensemen with 113 points

Recorded over 30 assists in a season six times

Recorded 52 goals and 351 points in 749 career games

and the club's fortunes began to change.

Dubnyk went 28–9–3 to finish the regular season and Minnesota ended up with 100 points and a wild-card spot in the playoffs. They beat the dominant St. Louis Blues in the first round before falling to the eventual Stanley Cup champions, the Chicago Blackhawks.

During his time with the Wild, Suter has become one of the best blue-liners in the NHL, leading his team's defensemen in points and assists in each of his three seasons in Minnesota. This type of excellent play should be more than enough to get him to the 2018 Winter Olympics for another shot at his dream of a gold medal.

FABULOUS FORWARDS

David
BACKES

RIGHT W

rick
NE

att
UCHEN

Jakub
VORACEK

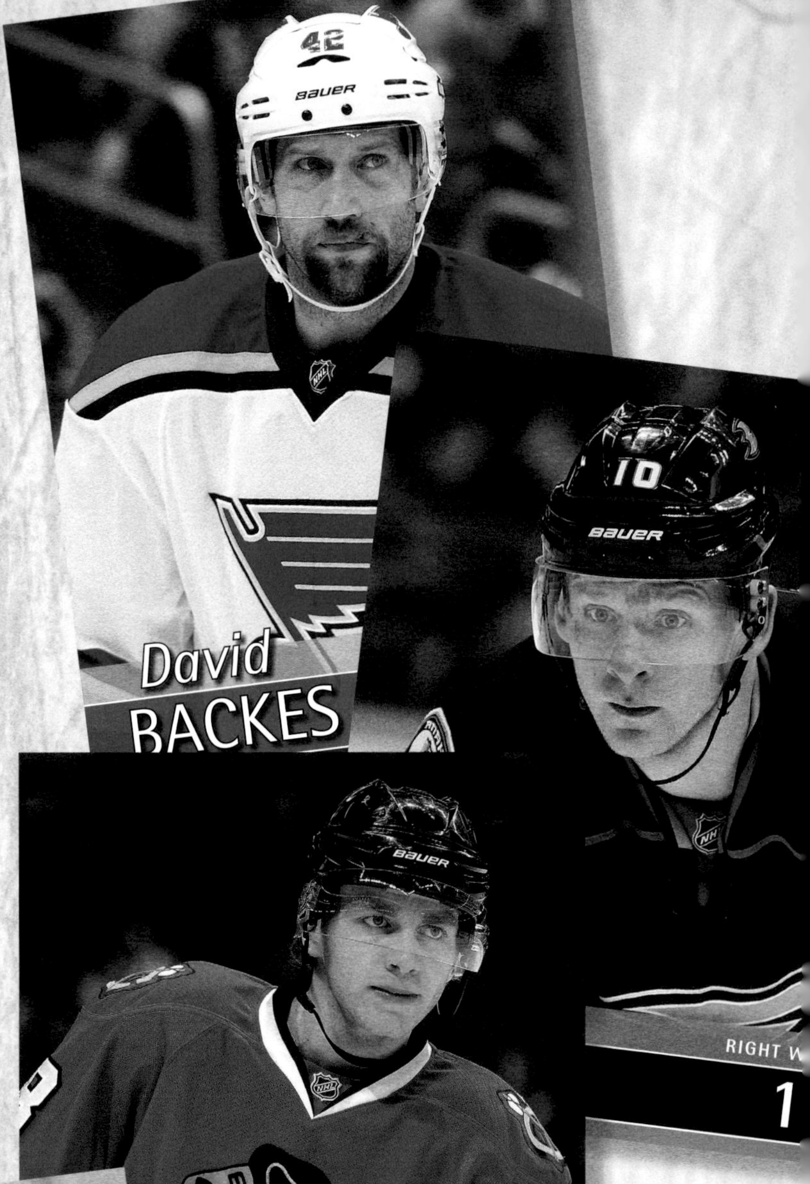

Gusto
NYQU

Loga
COUT

Jamie
BENN

TORONTO
MAPLE
LEAFS

CENTER

David
BACKES

CENTER
42

and didn't play an NHL game until December 19, 2006. He registered an assist in that game and a goal in the next, securing his spot with the big club. Over the course of the rest of the season, Backes racked up 23 points in 49 games and hasn't looked back since. For example, in his first year as captain, he totaled 54 points in 82 games, proving he was capable of handling the pressure and expectations that came with his new role.

Backes was a great choice to lead the St. Louis team because he plays a solid two-way game. He has recorded an average of 46 points per season over his nine-year career, with his highest of 62 coming in 2010–11. Backes does all of this while piling up about 100 penalty minutes per year (going over the 100-minute mark five times in his career to date). He plays an in-your-face style of game that is defensively sharp, making him a regular candidate for the Frank J. Selke Trophy, which goes to the best defensive forward (Backes was runner-up in 2012, losing to Patrice Bergeron). Backes is also one of the best faceoff men in the league, with a career average of about 50 percent. Simply put, he is the prototypical center that NHL teams love to have on their rosters, and despite not being a point-per-game player, Backes is the only active Blues player to make the franchise's all-time top 10 for points, goals and assists.

His athleticism and skill is often coupled with a power that is unstoppable. For instance, when the Blues went to Arizona to play the Coyotes on January 6, 2015, Backes made his opposition wish they had stayed home. St. Louis won the game 6–0, with Backes contributing four goals, all within a 17-minute span over the second and third periods.

Backes' successful season was an indicator of how well the Blues did in the 2014–15 regular campaign with 51 wins, second behind the New York Rangers' 53, and 109 points, which combined for first place in the Central Division. The team also had the fifth-best offense in the NHL with 248 goals scored. Ironically,

The St. Louis Blues have had a wide variety of players named as team captain since their inception in 1967. Many have been gritty, like Al Arbour or Brian Sutter; others have been highly skilled, such Red Berenson or Brett Hull; and then there were the all-round types of defensemen, such as Scott Stevens or Chris Pronger. Most recently, captain Eric Brewer was dealt away to the Tampa Bay Lightning before the Blues named David Backes as his successor on September 9, 2011, making Backes the 20th Blues leader in team history.

It was quite an accomplishment for the 6-foot-3, 221-pound Backes, who, at one point, was not even sure if he would ever play in the NHL. He was chosen in the second round of the 2003 entry draft by the Blues

they also took fifth place in goals allowed, which may have been the number one reason for their early playoff departure. The Blues were considered one of the favorites for the Stanley Cup prior to the start of the 2014–15 season, but unstable goal-tending knocked them down when it came to the postseason. The Minnesota Wild, a wild-card team, took the series in six games, and even though Backes was injured during the playoffs, he made no excuses for his poor play (only one goal and one assist). The Blues and Backes are quickly becoming known as regular-season wonders with no extra gear for the playoffs.

Backes acknowledged that the Blues have to start being as successful in the postseason as they are during the regular campaign. But, even considering the fact that the 31-year-old has spent his entire career in St. Louis, if the franchise decides to mix things up with a trade, he should have no problem finding a new club that will appreciate his skills, power and leadership, captaincy or not.

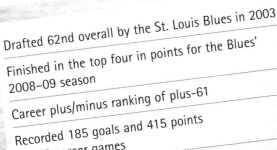

CAREER HIGHLIGHTS

Drafted 62nd overall by the St. Louis Blues in 2003

Finished in the top four in points for the Blues' 2008–09 season

Career plus/minus ranking of plus-61

Recorded 185 goals and 415 points in 648 career games

Nicklas
BACKSTROM 19
CENTER

When fans are asked to name the best centers in the NHL, Sidney Crosby, Jonathan Toews and Ryan Getzlaf are usually the players most commonly discussed. There is one player, however, who is often missing from these discussions, and that is Nicklas Backstrom of the Washington Capitals.

In the 2014–15 season, Backstrom led the league in assists with 60, and he has been in the top 10 in league points in four of his eight seasons since he first joined the Capitals in 2007–08 as a 20-year-old rookie. Backstrom still tends to fly under the radar, though, because he shares the ice with Alex Ovechkin, whose fondness for the spotlight has the ability to dwarf almost any player. Backstrom also may get less credit than some because the Washington club has fared poorly in the

playoffs. However, the Capitals believe Backstrom and Ovechkin, who are each inked to long-term contracts, are the pair that can lead the team to its first-ever Stanley Cup.

Drafted fourth overall in 2006, Backstrom exploded in his rookie year by racking up 69 points in 82 games and finished second to Patrick Kane in the Calder Memorial Trophy race. But what was quickly becoming obvious about Backstrom was his team-first attitude — 55 of those 69 points were assists. For a guy who regularly lines up with Ovechkin (who has been in the top 5 in goals scored in 9 of his 10 seasons), Backstrom has consistently demonstrated that he is an elite player who is willing to pass the puck. Highlighting this sense of partnership between the two players is the fact that Backstrom has assisted on more than 45 percent of Ovechkin's goals since the pair began playing together in 2007–08.

Backstrom's superb passing ability, great patience and instinct in reading the play are just a few of the qualities that prove he is especially valuable on the power play. For instance: Ovechkin's league-leading 25 power-play goals in 2014–15 were matched with Backstrom's league-leading 30 power-play assists. Backstrom's pass-first mentality means he doesn't score as many goals as he otherwise might, but goalies still need to be alert when he has the puck — Backstrom has an accurate shot when he chooses to use it. He has recorded over 60 assists in a season four times and produced a 101-point season in 2009–10 for fourth place in the league. During 2014–15, he collected his 419th assist to jump ahead of Michal Pivonka for the Capitals' all-time career assists record; Pivonka had set the record in 825 games, but the pass-first Backstrom achieved the milestone in only 562.

At 6-foot-1 and 210 pounds, Backstrom isn't undersized by any stretch of the imagination, but despite his stature, his game is built more on finesse and skating than on checking and aggression. He is disciplined, averaging only 37 penalty minutes a season and, as it is said in Washington, Ovechkin is rough enough for the both of them.

Almost a point-per-game player in the regular season (572 points in 577 games played through 2014–15), Backstrom drops off slightly in the playoffs, recording 51 points in 71 games. His production is still exemplary, as even the most hardened veteran scorers can buckle under playoff pressure. But the postseason disappointments are starting to mount in Washington, and Backstrom and Ovechkin are going to need to find another gear in order to produce when it matters most. In their 2015 playoff loss — a blown 3–1 series lead against the New York Rangers — Backstrom tallied only two assists in the seven-game campaign.

Many observers, including his teammates, think

Backstrom is too modest and as a result doesn't get the credit he really deserves. The 27-year-old prefers to look at team success rather than his own statistical output — a tendency that will always make him popular in the dressing room. But, if he can take his regular-season success into the postseason, Backstrom should finally get some long-overdue recognition as one of the league's best centers.

CAREER HIGHLIGHTS

Drafted 4th overall by the Washington Capitals in 2006

Ranked second in assists per game in Capitals' franchise history

Finished in the top-10 point leaders four times

Recorded 145 goals and 572 points in 577 career games

Jamie
BENN

LEFT WING

14

award, but what made the feat all the more note-worthy was that unbeknownst to fans, Benn had played his final regular-season game with a bad hip that required surgery. His strong work ethic also earned Benn a nomination for the Ted Lindsay Award for MVP as voted by the players.

Benn's hat trick versus the Predators was not the only one he had during the 2014–15 season. He scored three goals against the St. Louis Blues during a February contest, each goal showcasing the strengths of his all-round game. His first came less than three minutes into the game, proving why he has finished in the top-3 for goal scoring for four seasons as a Star; the second was a give-and-go with Jason Spezza (Benn scored, but his ability to assist on goals put him first on his team in 2014–15); and the third came on a power play during which Benn snapped the puck past the Blues' goaltender to show just why he has placed in the top 10 for power-play points every season in Dallas. This was Benn's first three-goal game and the Stars earned a win over a dominating Blues team.

If Dallas had more players like Benn, the Stars would have had a much better record than 41–31–10 in 2014–15, but their captain winning a major trophy like the Art Ross is definitely something to build on in the coming seasons.

As a bit of a late bloomer, Benn was drafted by the Stars 129th overall in 2007. Many teams had overlooked the native of Victoria, British Columbia, who went on to play junior hockey for two seasons with the Kelowna Rockets of the Western Hockey League (WHL) after being drafted. With the Rockets, Benn produced 147 points in 107 games and was a member of Team Canada at the 2009 World Junior Championships in Ottawa, where the team won gold. He was also a major reason why the Rockets went on to play in the 2009 Memorial Cup. The team didn't win the tournament, but Benn had an outstanding showing with a total of nine points in four games. He started the 2009–10 season as a

It was one of the wildest finishes to close out the NHL scoring race in many years and it ended with just nine seconds left in the last game of the year. Dallas Stars left-winger Jamie Benn had scored three times in the team's closing contest against the Nashville Predators, and even though these goals tied him in scoring with New York Islanders center John Tavares, it wasn't enough to take the lead. So while victory against the visiting Predators was inevitable, Benn's teammates kept feeding him the puck, hoping he would get one more point to claim the title. Finally, Cody Eakin put the puck in the net at 19:51 with assists from Trevor Daley and Benn.

Consequently, Benn took home the Art Ross Trophy, which was the first time a Dallas Star had ever won the

20-year-old playing with the big club in Dallas and he quickly proved he belonged. Benn played in all 82 games, scoring 22 goals (good for fourth on the team) and totaling 41 points. Dallas, however, missed the playoffs in 2010, so Benn was sent to the Texas Stars of the American Hockey League (AHL) for their post-season. Texas made it all the way to the Calder Cup finals, but lost in six games to the Hershey Bears. Despite the team's loss, Benn recorded 26 points in 24 games to close out his outstanding first year as a professional hockey player.

Outside of the lockout-shortened season in 2012–13, Benn has never produced less than 22 goals or 41 points in a season. The Stars have only made the playoffs once in Benn's six seasons with Dallas (a first-round exit against the Anaheim Ducks in 2014), but he still recorded five points in those six postseason games. Further, the team's future looks incredibly promising as general manager Jim Nill has added players like Tyler Seguin, John Klingberg and Jamie's brother, Jordie Benn, into the mix in the hopes that these driven young players can get Dallas back into playoff contention.

CAREER HIGHLIGHTS

Drafted 129th overall by the Dallas Stars in 2007

Named captain of the Dallas Stars in 2013

Member of the First All-Star Team for the 2013–14 season

Winner of the Art Ross Trophy in 2015

Recorded 151 goals and 359 points in 426 career games

Logan
COUTURE

CENTER
39

and in the dressing room. In a sink-or-swim situation, Couture floated above everyone else.

Couture was highly motivated at the start of the 2014–15 campaign because of the postseason loss to the Kings and the disappointment of missing out on being chosen for the Canadian Olympic Team in 2014 (the 6-foot-1, 195-pound center looked to be a sure bet to play in Sochi but a wrist injury forced him to remain a spectator). He still managed to finish the 2013–14 season with 53 points in 65 games but it was hard to miss out on a spot in the Olympics. Couture's strong comeback to start 2014 included playing in all 82 games and recording career highs in assists (40), points (67) and shots on goal (263). Despite his efforts, the Sharks missed the 2015 playoffs, but it appears the core of young players led by Couture has taken control of the San Jose club for the foreseeable future.

Couture first became a Shark when Wilson made a series of moves at the 2007 entry draft in order to take the youngster with the ninth overall pick. The Sharks were impressed with Couture's junior hockey career — he had posted 287 points in 232 games for the Ottawa 67's. Two years after being selected, Couture was assigned to the Worcester Sharks of the American Hockey League (AHL) where he quickly proved he was too good to stay in the minors with 53 points in 42 games. He was promoted to the San Jose club for his first full season in 2010–11 and recorded 56 points in 79 games (including 32 goals for second place on the team). His fine performance earned him a Calder Memorial Trophy nomination, but he came in second to Jeff Skinner.

Since his rookie year, Couture has remained a consistent producer and has never had less than 53 points in a full season. He has a terrific shot with lots of snap, but he also has soft hands when he gets into tight situations. Both highly competitive and composed, Couture is put to use in all situations and can score in any circumstance. He is industrious at even-strength as well as on the

The San Jose Sharks had their archrival Los Angeles Kings on the ropes with a lead of three games to none during the first round of the 2014 playoffs, but it all came apart when the Kings became one of four teams in league history to stage a miraculous postseason comeback to oust the reeling Sharks in seven games. The team's shock at their loss lingered into the next season, so general manager Doug Wilson decided they should start fresh by emphasizing their youthful players for the 2014–15 campaign. He got rid of veterans like Dan Boyle, Brad Stuart and Martin Havlat and did his best to reduce the leadership roles once held by Joe Thornton and Patrick Marleau. Instead, players like the 26-year-old Logan Couture were expected to take on a greater role both on the ice power play, with 89 career points with the extra man. As a result of his good play, Couture's ice time is now up to over 19 minutes per game and he is likely to be a team leader in this department, even though Todd McLellan has left as head coach.

Couture started a new venture during the 2014–15 season by becoming a contributor to ThePlayersTribune.com, a website founded by former baseball great Derek Jeter. Couture wrote about what it's like to go up against the other top centers in the league, including Sidney Crosby and Anze Kopitar. Some of Couture's most interesting comments were about the Detroit Red Wings' Pavel Datsyuk and how he made Couture a better athlete by forcing him to face the challenge of going up against one of the best players in the league.

Couture's challenge now is to help lead young Sharks like Barclay Goodrow, Tomas Hertl and Mirco Mueller toward becoming great NHL players. Luckily, there is no doubt that Couture is an excellent leader and role model who will take the Sharks into a bright future.

Drafted 9th overall by the San Jose Sharks in 2007

Selected to the First All-Rookie Team in 2010–11

Scored 29 career game-winning goals

Recorded 139 goals and 287 points in 379 career games

CAREER HIGHLIGHTS

Matt
DUCHENE

CENTER

9

coach Stan Butler, renowned for his ability to prepare young players for the NHL, pushed both Hodgson and Duchene to excellence. Duchene produced 129 points in 121 games for Brampton and helped lead the team to the OHL final in 2009. Despite his 26 points in 21 playoff games, the Windsor Spitfires ended the Battalion's hopes for a trip to the Memorial Cup tournament. The loss stung, but it didn't change the fact that Duchene was headed to the NHL.

The 2009 draft featured the sensational John Tavares and Victor Hedman, who went No. 1 and No. 2, respectively. Duchene, at No. 3, ended up in Colorado, which fulfilled a childhood dream — his signed Joe Sakic jersey with the Avalanche crest had always hung in the Duchene home while Matt was growing into a future NHL star.

Following all the hype of the draft and his sterling rookie season, Duchene avoided the sophomore slump, recording 27 goals and 67 points in 80 games in 2010–11. His third season, however, didn't go as planned, and ankle and knee injuries restricted Duchene to just 58 games. The injuries and subsequent break from action forced Duchene to look at his physical preparation to determine if the problems he encountered could be avoided in the future by training in different and more positive ways. As a result, Duchene stopped spending so much time in the weight room doing traditional lifting and instead focused on his core stability muscles. He also worked with training professionals to change his diet and to evaluate his skating stride.

Duchene left no stone unturned and returned from his injuries as a more explosive player with a renewed skating motion. His game and body were in greater sync than ever before. Unfortunately, his bounce-back campaign was delayed due to the lockout at the start of the 2012–13 season. He still managed to produce 43 points in 47 games of the shortened season, which tied him for the team lead, but the Avalanche were a horrible 16–25–7 and finished fifth in the Northwest Division.

Matt Duchene had a great rookie campaign. The third overall pick in the 2009 draft was a difference-maker for his Colorado Avalanche team, jumping into the league as an 18-year-old and scoring 24 goals and 55 points to lead all rookies. Topping off this excellent first season, he also ended up making the 2009–10 First All-Rookie Team and finishing third in Calder Memorial Trophy voting behind defenseman Tyler Myers of the Buffalo Sabres and goaltender Jimmy Howard of the Detroit Red Wings.

Duchene's road to the NHL started in the Ontario Hockey League (OHL), playing for the Brampton Battalion as a top junior player. The native of Haliburton, Ontario, was fortunate to have childhood friend Cody Hodgson as a teammate, and Brampton

The next season saw a dramatic shift in Colorado's fortunes when new coach Patrick Roy instilled some fire into his group. Duchene recorded 70 points (a career high) and led his team in assists for the second consecutive year. The Avalanche took the top spot in the Central Division with 112 points, which was their best finish since 2000–01 when they won the Cup. Colorado was knocked out of the playoffs in the first round, but Duchene's strong play landed him a spot on the 2014 Canadian Olympic team that ended up winning gold.

Duchene played well in 2014–15, but his point total dropped to 55 even though he skated in all 82 games. The Avalanche also dropped, as the group who some say over-achieved the previous year came back down to earth. Duchene, however, was named to Team Canada for the 2015 World Championships, and he helped the team take gold by recording

12 points in 10 games, making him the fifth-highest point producer in the entire tournament. This type of fine play has set Duchene up for a starring role with Colorado in the 2015–16 season and beyond.

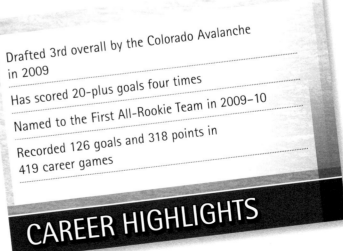

Drafted 3rd overall by the Colorado Avalanche in 2009

Has scored 20-plus goals four times

Named to the First All-Rookie Team in 2009–10

Recorded 126 goals and 318 points in 419 career games

CAREER HIGHLIGHTS

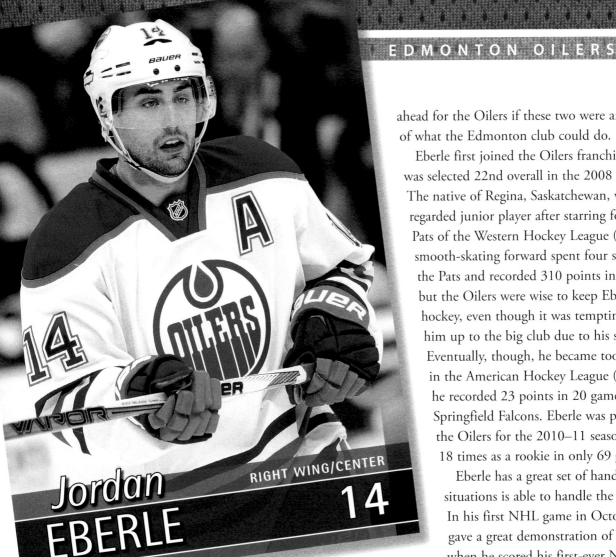

Jordan
EBERLE

RIGHT WING/CENTER

14

ahead for the Oilers if these two were any indication of what the Edmonton club could do.

Eberle first joined the Oilers franchise when he was selected 22nd overall in the 2008 entry draft. The native of Regina, Saskatchewan, was a highly regarded junior player after starring for the Regina Pats of the Western Hockey League (WHL). The smooth-skating forward spent four seasons with the Pats and recorded 310 points in 254 games, but the Oilers were wise to keep Eberle in junior hockey, even though it was tempting to bring him up to the big club due to his superb playing. Eventually, though, he became too skilled to stay in the American Hockey League (AHL), where he recorded 23 points in 20 games for the Springfield Falcons. Eberle was promoted to the Oilers for the 2010–11 season and scored 18 times as a rookie in only 69 games played.

Eberle has a great set of hands and in tight situations is able to handle the puck with ease. In his first NHL game in October 2010, he gave a great demonstration of these skills when he scored his first-ever NHL goal.

The Oilers were playing the Calgary Flames, and when Eberle was part of the penalty-killers, he managed to get the puck out of his own end and into the offensive zone, moving it past veteran defenseman Ian White. Eberle deked goalie Miikka Kiprusoff out of position to deposit a shorthanded goal into the Calgary net. Eberle added a power-play assist on another Oilers goal in the 4–0 win and was named the first star of the game to complete his memorable debut. He scored another shorthanded goal later that month to lead the team with two for the season.

In the years that have followed, Eberle has not stopped scoring, leading the Oilers in points for three of his five seasons with the team. His best season came in his second NHL campaign in 2011–12, when he had 34 goals and 76 points in 78 games. He also led the Edmonton team in power-play points in 2013–14 and 2014–15, proving he has grown into a more

There's nothing like playing hockey with the best players from around the world to put a terrible NHL season out of your mind. At the end of the 2014–15 season, Jordan Eberle was coming off another bad run with the Edmonton Oilers (who had won only 24 games and recorded just 62 points), and he needed to reinvigorate his confidence. He did so at the 2015 IIHF World Hockey Championships in Prague, ending up with 13 points in 10 games on the way to winning Canada's gold medal. Eberle's timing was impeccable because Canada's coach, Todd McLellan, was soon after named the new bench boss for the Oilers. McLellan went out of his way to say that Eberle and teammate Taylor Hall had shown him their desire to succeed in the NHL, which made him believe that better days are productive player.

Eberle is not the aggressive sort and has only 90 penalty minutes in five seasons. His sportsmanship and gentlemanly behavior earned him a nomination for the Lady Byng Memorial Trophy in 2012, but he finished second to Brian Campbell of the Florida Panthers by only 4 percent. Eberle is also not a big guy at 5-foot-11, 180 pounds, but he has a solid build that he uses to his advantage by fearlessly going to the net whenever he can.

Eberle has found good chemistry with Hall, and in 2015–16 they will both be playing with junior sensation Connor McDavid. If he joins them at center, it could be the making of a super-line, and that is an exciting thought for Eberle to contemplate as he prepares for the upcoming season.

CAREER HIGHLIGHTS

Drafted 22nd overall by the Edmonton Oilers in 2008

Three-time gold-medal-winner with Team Canada at three different levels of hockey

Led the Oilers in points three times (2010–11, 2011–12 and 2014–15)

Recorded 120 goals and 284 points in 356 career games

Patrick KANE

RIGHT WING

88

begin. He was on board as the Blackhawks beat the Nashville Predators in six games and then took out the Minnesota Wild and Anaheim Ducks in the next two rounds. The Tampa Bay Lightning proved to be a tough opponent in the Stanley Cup final and were leading the series after three games. Lightning defenseman Victor Hedman stalked Kane closely and he was left off the score sheet for over 220 minutes before assisting on Brandon Saad's game-winning goal in the third period of Game 4. The Blackhawks won the next contest to force Game 6 back in Chicago for their chance to win the Cup on home ice for the first time since 1938. This was Kane's time to shine: he set up Duncan Keith with the opening point of the game and later netted his first goal of the series with five minutes left in the third. The Lightning couldn't recover and the Blackhawks won their third Cup in six years.

Kane ended up tied for the most points in the playoffs with 23, proving that he is a clutch hockey player who can score and set up goals at opportune times — especially in the playoffs, where he has recorded 114 points in 116 games.

The 5-foot-11, 181-pound Kane has been a remarkably consistent performer since joining the NHL in 2007–08. He won the Calder Memorial Trophy as the NHL's best rookie with 72 points in 82 games (a team-leading total as well) and he quickly mastered how to play in the league at his size. He is almost a point-per-game player with 557 points in 576 games.

In 2009–10, Kane notched 88 points, earned himself the honor of being named to the First All-Star Team and won his first Stanley Cup by scoring the championship-winning goal in overtime against the Philadelphia Flyers. Kane continued to perform well in the regular season and playoffs, but he really proved himself in the 2013 postseason when he put up 19 points in 23 games, including a league-leading nine even-strength goals, on his way to a second Stanley Cup. His inspiring

When Patrick Kane suffered a serious injury in February 2015, everyone thought he would miss the rest of the regular season, as well as most of the playoffs, provided the Chicago Blackhawks progressed that far. Up until the time of his injury, Kane had been enjoying one of his best years in the NHL with 64 points in 61 games and had a great chance of winning his first-ever Art Ross Trophy. However, when he fell awkwardly into the boards during a game against the Florida Panthers, it was discovered that his broken left clavicle required surgery. Kane's season was put on hold and the Blackhawks started to wonder if they could get anywhere in the playoffs without their best scorer.

Much to everyone's surprise, Kane was ready to play by the time the first round of the playoffs was about to

accomplishments earned him the Conn Smythe Trophy for MVP of the playoffs.

All of this success should come as no surprise, considering Kane's start in hockey. The native of Buffalo played for four seasons in the USA Hockey National Team Development Program, recording 172 points in 121 games. He then played one season with the London Knights of the Ontario Hockey League (OHL) where he led in points with 145. It's no wonder the Blackhawks took him first overall in 2007, especially considering he won the OHL rookie of the year award.

Kane is the only active player in the top 10 on the Blackhawks' list of all-time leaders in points (557). He is also fourth in franchise playoff points (114), is a Lady Byng Memorial Trophy runner-up (2013) and has combined with teammate Jonathan Toews for over 1,000 points in their eight

seasons playing together — all before the age of 27. It is exciting for hockey fans to see that such a tremendous effort has been rewarded with an impressive hockey career that promises more greatness to come.

Drafted 1st overall by the Chicago Blackhawks in 2007

One of seven Blackhawks players to win three Stanley Cups in six years

Winner of the Conn Smythe Trophy in 2013

Recorded 205 goals and 557 points in 576 career games

CAREER HIGHLIGHTS

RIGHT WING

Phil
KESSEL

81

about to sign a contract with the Nashville Predators. He had put up three respectable seasons with the Boston Bruins, so Brian Burke, Toronto's general manager at the time, was determined to land the high-scoring Kessel and outbid Nashville. Burke did so and Kessel responded well to his new franchise, finishing in the top 10 in league scoring for three consecutive seasons — the only other Maple Leafs player to do so in the modern NHL was franchise great and Hall of Famer Darryl Sittler.

Toronto fans, however, like their stars with a bit of grit. "Sandpaper" is an adjective often used to describe this rugged, dogged style of play, and unfortunately for Kessel, he didn't often display these qualities in Toronto. He hit the back of the net regularly, but Leafs diehards missed the tooth-and-nail effort they are used to seeing from former Maple Leaf stars Wendel Clark, Doug Gilmour and Darcy Tucker. It's actually quite possible that Kessel is more talented than all of these men, but he just didn't look like he came to the arena ready to give a pint of blood to win the game. Even though that attitude might not matter on the score sheet, it definitely mattered to Leafs fans who endlessly "bleed blue."

In his defense, it's difficult to always put the best foot forward in a full 82-game season (which he has done four times), but Kessel is still undoubtedly one of the best forwards in the NHL. He has blazing speed (proven at the NHL All-Star Skills Competition when he came in third for fastest skater) and an incredibly accurate shot that he can whip into the smallest of openings to score goals. He also led the Leafs in points in each of the six seasons he was with the club, with a career-high 82 in 2011–12 and 80 in 2013–14. He was the only active Maple Leaf on the franchise's top 10 all-time leaders list for game-winning goals (31), shots on goal (1,663) and power-play goals (52). Kessel also led his team with four goals during their 2013 playoff stint.

Despite his personal achievements, the 2014–15 season unraveled for the Maple Leafs when the team

Phil Kessel attracts an extraordinary amount of attention for a player who doesn't like the media. That's not to say he hates the spotlight — scoring goals and drawing the coverage of opposing team's top defenders is something any elite hockey player craves — but the weight of the expectation to thrive on a struggling team in a city with an unforgiving media market created a hostile environment for the star. His solution seemed to be to avoid the media and let his game do the talking. Unfortunately, his game suffered from a quiet spell and his contract with the Toronto Maple Leafs that garnered him $10 million in 2014–15 became a lightning rod for the media and fans who expected more from the All-Star winger.

Before signing with the Leafs in 2009, Kessel was

went through a mid-season coaching change, though Kessel still managed 25 goals and 61 points. Hockey critics insinuated that Kessel had a "lack of character," but many forgot just how difficult it was for the gifted winger to even be in the NHL at all, considering he had a cancer scare early on in his pro career. There is no way Kessel could have thrived in the ultra-competitive NHL, as well as had the courage to fight off a killer disease, without having the constitution of a winner.

Kessel is undoubtedly a talented hockey player, but Toronto was not the right city for him to play in. His athletic skills will thrive on his new team, the Pittsburgh Penguins, where he doesn't have to be the center of attention because his teammates, like Sidney Crosby and Evgeni Malkin, are already the stars. Kessel just has to do what he has always done best: put the puck in the net.

Drafted 5th overall by the Boston Bruins in 2006

Winner of the Bill Masterton Memorial Trophy in 2006–07

Led in points for six consecutive seasons with the Maple Leafs (2009–10 to 2014–15)

Recorded 247 goals and 520 points in 668 career games

CAREER HIGHLIGHTS

CENTER

Anze
KOPITAR   11

If Los Angeles Kings center Anze Kopitar scored more goals, his name would come up much more often in the discussion surrounding the best players in the NHL. He has scored over 30 goals twice in his nine-year career, but he is more likely to settle in at around 25 goals during an average NHL season. Close observers, however, will note that the 6-foot-3, 224-pound Kopitar is one of the best two-way players in the league and belongs among names like Sidney Crosby, Jonathan Toews, John Tavares, Alex Ovechkin and Jamie Benn for best-player accolades. Kopitar's excellence is also certainly appreciated by his teammates, who have seen him play some of his best hockey during two successful runs at the Stanley Cup.

The fact that Kopitar is even playing in the NHL is

something of a miracle considering he was born in the small town of Jesenice, Slovenia. A young Kopitar dreamed of playing hockey in the far-away NHL, so he practiced his English off the ice while his father Matjaz served as his on-ice hockey hero. Kopitar watched as his dad celebrated a string of local championships, victories that served to fuel Kopitar's desire to make the NHL and take home its ultimate prize — the Stanley Cup.

Matjaz did what many North American parents do — he created a backyard rink for his two boys. Younger brother Gasper served as goalie for Kopitar and it wasn't long before Kopitar's scoring exploits were something of a local legend. A poster of Wayne Gretzky in his Los Angeles Kings uniform hung in the boys' bedroom and provided further motivation to make it to the top level of professional hockey. So when it became obvious that Kopitar was ready to move on from Slovenia, he relocated to Sweden at age 15 to further develop his skills.

Kopitar was an offensive powerhouse in Sweden and at 17 years old, he won a scoring title with 49 points in 30 games. His excellent play made him one of Europe's top junior prospects, which got him noticed by none other than the Los Angeles Kings. They selected Kopitar 11th overall in the 2005 entry draft and his father was naturally overcome with emotion. He officially joined the Kings as a 19-year-old in 2006–07, after having never played a game in the minors.

After scoring two goals versus the Anaheim Ducks in his first NHL game, Kopitar quickly established himself as a quality player and has produced no fewer than 61 points in any full NHL season. He has not yet won an NHL award, but is perpetually in consideration for more than one trophy, including the Hart Memorial Trophy, the Lady Byng Memorial Trophy and the Frank J. Selke Trophy (he received his first official nomination for the Byng and second for the Selke in 2014–15). Individual recognition aside, Kopitar has contributed significantly to his team, helping the Kings win two championships. He was a superb performer in the 2012 postseason with 20 points in 20 games when the Kings took their first-ever Stanley Cup, and again in 2014 when he had 26 points in 26 games for their second. Kopitar also takes great pride in his defensive work, as he is a career plus-45 in the regular season and plus-22 in the postseason.

In 2014–15, the hard-working center led his team in points (64) for the eighth consecutive regular season, but the defending Kings managed to miss the playoffs. On the Kings' career leaders list, Kopitar sits in seventh for points, fourth for game-winning goals and eighth for power-play goals. He has also only missed 21 games in his entire nine-year career, showing he is willing to put in the work to keep his place in the NHL, no matter how much success he already has. With numbers like these, fans can look forward to the many more accomplishments Kopitar will achieve in the future.

Drafted 11th overall by the Los Angeles Kings in 2005

Member of two Stanley Cup–winning teams in 2012 and 2014

Recorded 18 goals and 60 points in 70 career playoff games

Recorded 218 goals and 610 points in 683 career games

CAREER HIGHLIGHTS

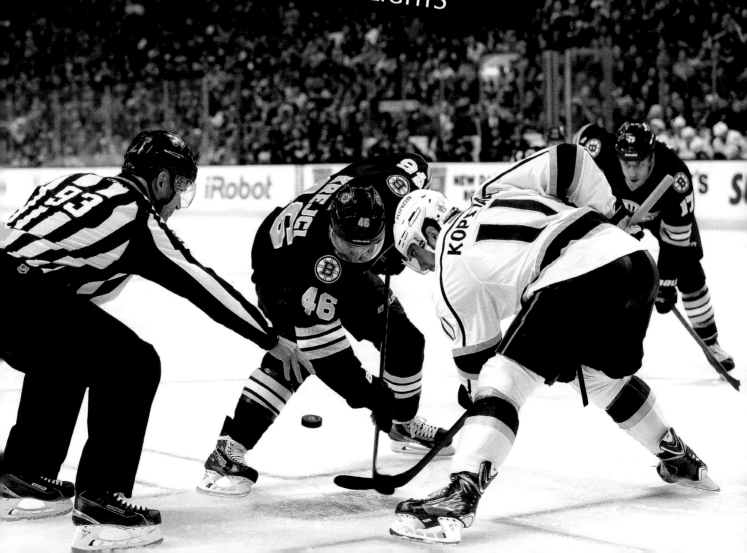

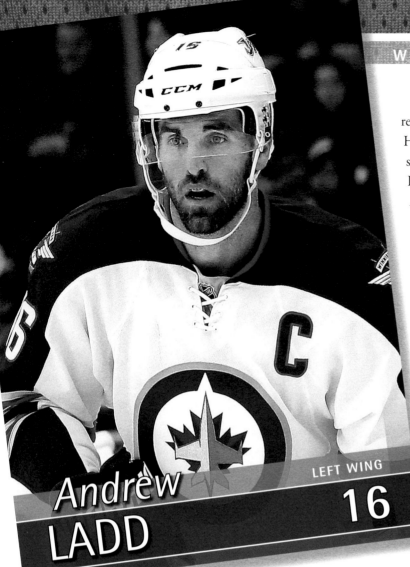

Andrew
LADD

LEFT WING

16

returning to the WHL, this time with the Calgary Hitmen, where he collected 75 points in the 2003–04 season, good enough for 15th in league scoring.

In 2004, Ladd was awarded the WHL Plus-Minus Award for going an impressive plus-39. This success led to Ladd being drafted fourth overall by the Carolina Hurricanes in the 2004 NHL entry draft and having the opportunity to join Team Canada at the 2005 World Junior Championships, where he helped his team win gold.

After a short stint with the Lowell Lock Monsters of the American Hockey League (AHL), the Hurricanes called Ladd up to the big leagues in November 2005. Despite being sidelined with a knee injury and sent down again that same season, Ladd ended up back with Carolina for the postseason, just in time to help the franchise secure its first-ever Stanley Cup title. Ladd had only played in 29 regular-season games, but participated in 17 of 25 playoff games, helping the cause with five points.

The 29-year-old Maple Ridge, British Columbia, native was eventually dealt to Chicago in 2008 after two unproductive years in Carolina. This trade was in exchange for Tuomo Ruutu, and it turned out to be a great deal for Chicago, as Ladd found his game again in the Windy City.

Ladd played a big part on the Chicago championship team, and when he hoisted the Stanley Cup over his head for the second time in just five seasons, he had chipped in 38 points during the 2009–10 regular season and added six more in the playoffs. However, he was once again forced to move — this time to the Atlanta Thrashers for the 2010–11 season where he was named team captain. The Atlanta-based franchise moved north of the border in time for the 2011–12 season, and in Canada was revived as the Winnipeg Jets.

The Jets have yet to celebrate an NHL title, but having a player like Ladd has certainly helped. He led the team in points with 62 for the 2014–15 season, which was also a career high. His 38 assists (another

Just after the Chicago Blackhawks won the Stanley Cup in 2010, the team had to make some difficult choices. Salary-cap issues forced the Blackhawks to deal away Kris Versteeg, Dustin Byfuglien and others in order to meet the requirements for the next season. Six-foot-two, 205-pound winger Andrew Ladd also left in a deal, as he was sent to the Atlanta Thrashers. This marked the second time Ladd had to leave a Stanley Cup–winning team. Nonetheless, his 10-year career with four different franchises has been marked with consistent success.

After a successful start in Junior A hockey, Ladd was drafted into the Western Hockey League (WHL) by the Vancouver Giants. He went back to the British Columbia Hockey League (BCHL) for a season before

career-high) provided the drive the Jets needed as they made the postseason for the first time since the original Jets' 1995–96 season. His impressive year included 24 goals (six of which were game-winners), 72 penalty minutes and a team-leading time on ice (over 1,600 minutes), all while appearing in 81 games. Ladd's stand-out season was further recognized when he was one of three players selected as a finalist for the 2014–15 Mark Messier NHL Leadership Award, which is given to the player who exemplifies great leadership qualities to his team during the regular season.

Despite the team's exciting chase to snag the second Western Conference wild-card playoff spot, their exhaustion began to show. Coupled with key injuries and constant pressure from the Anaheim Ducks, the Jets were swept during the first round.

But now that he is firmly entrenched in a new city, Ladd can focus on leading the team on an upward trend. His current contract is a five-year deal worth $22 million, which indicates that Winnipeg management believes good veterans like Ladd are impor-tant to the Jets' future success. Winnipeg has many top prospects waiting for a spot on the team, and this future collection of players may indeed help Ladd lift the Stanley Cup for a third time.

Drafted 4th overall by the Carolina Hurricanes in 2004

Member of two Stanley Cup–winning teams

Named team captain of the Atlanta Thrashers in 2010

Recorded 185 goals and 420 points in 691 career games

CAREER HIGHLIGHTS

Evgeni
MALKIN

CENTER
71

Memorial Trophy (league MVP in 2012), the Ted Lindsay Award (league MVP as voted by the players in 2012), three First All-Star Team selections (in 2008, 2009 and 2012) and a pair of Art Ross trophies (in 2009 and 2012 for top point-scorer). His name is also on the Stanley Cup after a superb performance in the 2009 postseason that saw him record 36 points in 24 games, earning him yet another award — the Conn Smythe Trophy that is given to the MVP of the playoffs. Further, Malkin has a gold medal from the 2012 World Championships where he scored an amazing 19 points in 10 games playing for Russia.

Another look at his resume shows that Malkin has only been able to play a full season twice in his entire career due to recurring injuries. He also couldn't score a goal in his final 10 games of the 2014–15 regular season and was completely pointless in the 2015 playoffs where the Penguins were knocked out in five games by the New York Rangers. Oddly, the Penguins' general manager Jim Rutherford insisted that Malkin had an injured ankle during the postseason, but the Pittsburgh center went to Prague a few weeks later to play for Russia in the World Championships. He scored key goals against Sweden and the United States to help Russia advance to the gold-medal game, and he notched Russia's only goal (his fifth of the tournament) in the final contest, a 6–1 defeat to Canada. His excellent play and contribution to the silver medal solidified the 29-year-old's ability to come back to elite status in hockey.

Malkin is a big man at 6-foot-3, so he can play the power-forward position well, but he can also display great finesse with the puck. His occasional edginess can get him into penalty trouble (he has a career average of 65 minutes a season), but any impressive goal-scorer needs to assert himself once in a while in order to get room on the ice. Malkin's skills also include his ability to breeze by defenders with speed before deking the netminder. When he is determined to score, there is

The Pittsburgh Penguins' Evgeni Malkin is one of the best players the NHL has ever seen, but he had to fight for his right to play hockey in North America. After growing up in Magnitogorsk, Russia, where he played junior hockey from age 16 to 20, his home country didn't want to lose him to the Penguins, who had drafted him second overall in 2004. Malkin had to jump through various legal hoops between 2006 and 2007 in order to finally gain the opportunity to play unencumbered in Pittsburgh.

It's a good thing too because a quick look at his resume shows that during Malkin's nine-year NHL career, he has accomplished more than most players ever will. His long list of achievements include the Calder Memorial Trophy (best rookie in 2007), the Hart

virtually no way to stop Malkin's excellent shot. He has only one 50-goal season to his credit and could have had more, but quality linemates are hard to come by in Pittsburgh, a team with a top-heavy payroll that eats up most of the salary cap (Malkin alone makes over $9 million a season). Overall, the Penguins were below the 2014–15 league average in goals for (the last time this happened was in 2005–06), but they did manage to maintain their excellent penalty-kill percentage (84.4), as well as place ninth in goals against thanks to Marc-Andre Fleury's solid goaltending.

The Penguins had a new coach for the 2014–15 season and many questioned if Mike Johnston was the right man for the job considering the Penguins *just* made the playoffs

with 98 points for a wild-card spot. The opinion also exists that Malkin should be traded to obtain prospects and draft choices while unloading a major salary. While that might seem like a good idea on paper, the odds are slim that the Penguins will let go of one of the most accomplished players in the NHL.

Drafted 2nd overall by the Pittsburgh Penguins in 2004

Recorded 111 points in 101 career playoff games

Holds 12th place in points per game for all-time leaders

Recorded 268 goals and 702 points in 587 career games

CAREER HIGHLIGHTS

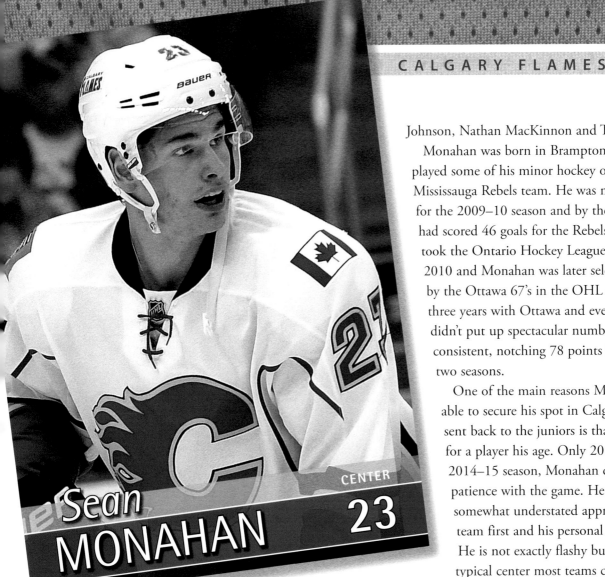

Sean
MONAHAN
CENTER
23

Johnson, Nathan MacKinnon and Tyler Toffoli.

Monahan was born in Brampton, Ontario, and played some of his minor hockey on the nearby Mississauga Rebels team. He was named their captain for the 2009–10 season and by the time he left, he had scored 46 goals for the Rebels. His team also took the Ontario Hockey League (OHL) Cup in 2010 and Monahan was later selected 16th overall by the Ottawa 67's in the OHL draft. He played three years with Ottawa and even though he didn't put up spectacular numbers, he was always consistent, notching 78 points in each of his last two seasons.

One of the main reasons Monahan has been able to secure his spot in Calgary and not get sent back to the juniors is that he is so mature for a player his age. Only 20 years old in the 2014–15 season, Monahan displayed a veteran's patience with the game. He has a quiet and somewhat understated approach that puts the team first and his personal objectives second. He is not exactly flashy but he is the proto-typical center most teams crave. His accurate shot gave him a 15.7 shooting percentage in his first year, the best on the team for anyone shooting more than 70 times on goal. He improved to 16.2 in 2014–15 and led all forwards with an average time-on-ice of 19:37. Monahan also committed himself to playing a two-way game and raised his plus/minus from minus-20 as a rookie to plus-8 in his second year.

If there is such a thing as the sophomore jinx, Monahan avoided it when he came on even stronger in 2014–15. He finished with 31 goals, 31 assists and eight game-winning goals that tied him for the third-best mark in the NHL. He centered a line that featured veteran winger Jiri Hudler and together they totaled 62 goals and 138 points.

Coming into 2014–15, the Flames were not expected to be in the playoff hunt. As a young, inexperienced squad with question marks at key positions, many experts figured the team to be on the outside looking

When Sean Monahan was made the sixth-overall pick by the Calgary Flames at the 2013 NHL entry draft, he proclaimed he was ready to make the team on his first try. Monahan's bravado was nothing new for an early first-rounder, but not many can actually back it up.

Not only did Monahan prove he belonged in the NHL, he was one of the better players on the Flames' roster during the 2013–14 season. He had an assist in his debut game and scored six goals in his first eight games to help give the Flames a large boost of energy. Monahan's attention-grabbing start kept him with the team for the whole season and he produced a respectable 22 goals and 34 points in 75 games, good for eighth place in rookie scoring in a year with players like Tyler

in before Christmas had even arrived. But, led by Monahan's solid play, many Flames had their coming-out parties in 2014–15 and Calgary was the surprise of the league. The club finished with 45 wins and knocked off the Vancouver Canucks in the first round of the postseason. What was glaringly obvious in Round 2 was the size advantage the Anaheim Ducks had on the Flames, and while Monahan will never be a bruiser, adding some strength to his game is sure to be a goal for the future.

The Flames appear to have a good season ahead of them with a rejuvenated roster of young players like Monahan, Sam Bennett, Johnny Gaudreau and the major acquisition of defenseman Dougie Hamilton

Drafted 6th overall by the Calgary Flames in 2013

Named the MVP of the OHL Cup in 2010

Tied for third in the NHL with eight game-winning goals in 2014–15

Recorded 53 goals and 96 points in 156 career games

CAREER HIGHLIGHTS

from the Boston Bruins. Many believe the team will take one step back before taking another forward, but this could be an underestimation as the Flames make big strides for their future success — with Monahan leading the charge.

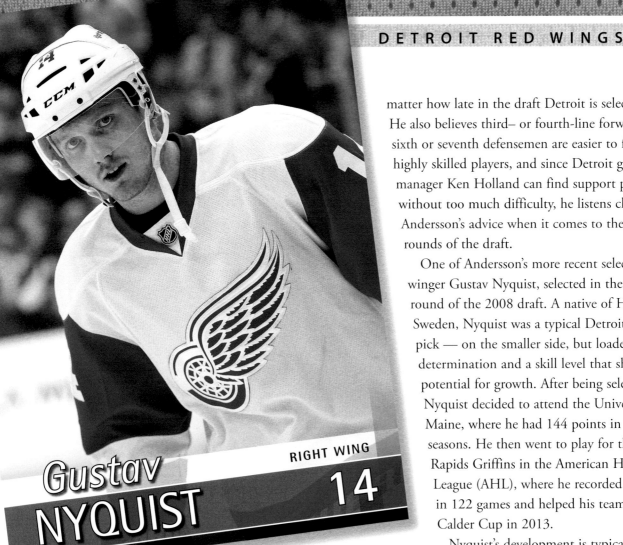

Gustav
NYQUIST

RIGHT WING

14

matter how late in the draft Detroit is selecting. He also believes third– or fourth-line forwards and sixth or seventh defensemen are easier to find than highly skilled players, and since Detroit general manager Ken Holland can find support players without too much difficulty, he listens closely to Andersson's advice when it comes to the later rounds of the draft.

One of Andersson's more recent selections is winger Gustav Nyquist, selected in the fourth round of the 2008 draft. A native of Halmstad, Sweden, Nyquist was a typical Detroit late-round pick — on the smaller side, but loaded with determination and a skill level that showed potential for growth. After being selected, Nyquist decided to attend the University of Maine, where he had 144 points in three seasons. He then went to play for the Grand Rapids Griffins in the American Hockey League (AHL), where he recorded 122 points in 122 games and helped his team win the Calder Cup in 2013.

Nyquist's development is typical of what the Red Wings do to make their prospects NHL-ready. Nyquist also knew he would benefit from playing college hockey in the United States, where he could both practice hockey as well as complete his education. Soon after his final year with the Griffins, Nyquist was officially promoted to the Red Wings, and during the 2013–14 season led the team in goals with 28, even though he only played in 57 NHL games that year. His performance came as a bit of a surprise because he had scored just four times in 40 games when called up in the two previous seasons. Nyquist, however, showed he had a sharp eye for shooting with an 18.3 shooting percentage, which was good for fourth in the league in 2013–14. This skill also helped him score six game-winning goals, another team-leading statistic.

The 2014–15 season saw Nyquist get off to a fast start as he built on his productive season the year before. He managed a career-high 54 points, including

H akan Andersson isn't exactly a household name among hockey fans, but he is definitely an important person to the Detroit Red Wings. Andersson is the Director of European Scouting for the Michigan franchise, and, consequently, the club owes a lot of its success to him. The super-scout's input had led the Red Wings to draft some great hockey players like Henrik Zetterberg, Pavel Datsyuk, Johan Franzen and Niklas Kronwall, all of whom have won the Stanley Cup with the winged wheel on their sweater. Andersson rarely has a first-round draft choice to ponder since the Red Wings have made the playoffs for the last 24 years (only Kronwall was selected in the top 30 of the entry draft), but that is what makes his style so unique. As far as Andersson is concerned, skill rules the day, no

14 power-play goals — the third-highest total in the league that season. But the 25-year-old's best moment came in a game against the Ottawa Senators on December 27, 2014. He held the puck on his stick for a total of 28 seconds, circling the Senators' net three times and fighting off several Ottawa players before finally taking a shot through traffic to beat Senators goaltender Craig Anderson from about 30 feet out and giving the Red Wings a 3–2 overtime victory. It was one the most spectacular goals of the NHL season.

Former Detroit coach Mike Babcock loved Nyquist's good shot and hockey sense, but now that Babcock has left for the Toronto Maple Leafs, Nyquist is again under the watchful eye of Jeff Blashill, who mentored the 5-foot-11, 183-pound winger in Grand Rapids. Nyquist is incredibly talented, but still has room to improve, especially in the postseason (he only has seven points in 30 playoff games). Being paired with his

Calder Cup–winning coach may bring back Nyquist's postseason drive.

Thanks to the talent from Nyquist and other Red Wings recruits, such as Tomas Tatar, Jonathan Ericsson and goalie Petr Mrazek, Detroit's future appears to be bright. Special thanks to Hakan Andersson too, of course.

CAREER HIGHLIGHTS

Drafted 121st overall by the Detroit Red Wings in 2008

Won the silver medal with Sweden at the 2014 Winter Olympics

Led Detroit in goals scored with 28 in 2013–14

Recorded 59 goals and 115 points in 179 career games

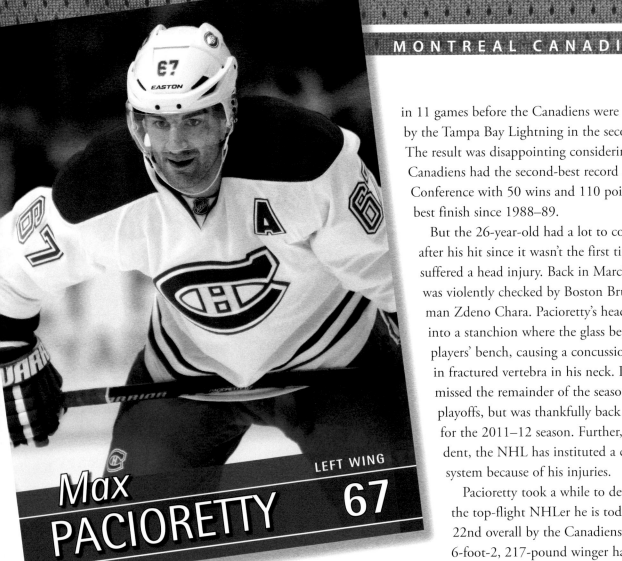

LEFT WING

Max
PACIORETTY 67

in 11 games before the Canadiens were knocked out by the Tampa Bay Lightning in the second round. The result was disappointing considering that the Canadiens had the second-best record in the Eastern Conference with 50 wins and 110 points — their best finish since 1988–89.

But the 26-year-old had a lot to contemplate after his hit since it wasn't the first time he had suffered a head injury. Back in March 2011, he was violently checked by Boston Bruins defenseman Zdeno Chara. Pacioretty's head was rammed into a stanchion where the glass began next to the players' bench, causing a concussion and resulting in fractured vertebra in his neck. Pacioretty missed the remainder of the season and the playoffs, but was thankfully back to full health for the 2011–12 season. Further, since the incident, the NHL has instituted a curved-glass system because of his injuries.

Pacioretty took a while to develop into the top-flight NHLer he is today. Drafted 22nd overall by the Canadiens in 2007, the 6-foot-2, 217-pound winger had little impact in Montreal in his first three seasons, recording only 49 points total. He had the skill set, but seemed to be overwhelmed by the speed of the NHL game. He had played high school hockey in his home state of Connecticut before signing on for one season in the United States Hockey League (USHL) for the Sioux City Musketeers, where he had 63 points in 60 games. Then he moved on to the University of Michigan for one year in 2007–08 before turning professional with Montreal's farm team, the Hamilton Bulldogs. In a three-year period with the Bulldogs, Pacioretty had 72 points in 82 games and looked ready to contribute at the NHL level.

The injury suffered at the hands of Chara held Pacioretty to just 37 games in 2010–11, but he came back stronger the following year and broke out into the star he is now known as. He accumulated 33 goals, led his team with 65 points and was awarded the Bill

It was a scary moment in the Montreal Canadiens' 80th game of the 2014–15 season. Just over five minutes into the contest, Montreal left-winger Max Pacioretty was hit by the Florida Panthers' Dmitry Kulikov and then clipped skates with Panther Alex Petrovic before awkwardly falling backward into the boards. It was just a slight hip check (although Kulikov was assessed a penalty), but Pacioretty was visibly shaken by the contact. He missed the final two games of the regular season and the first game of the playoffs, but was back for Game 2, scoring a power-play goal in Montreal's 3–2 win.

After being slammed into the boards in Florida, Pacioretty was determined to come back and help his team win in the postseason. He recorded seven points

Masterton Memorial Trophy for his perseverance and dedication to the game of hockey. The 2013–14 season saw even more improvements for Pacioretty with a career-high 39 goals, a league-leading 11 game-winning goals and 11 points in 17 playoff games. All of this success proved that over the years, Pacioretty had developed into a consistent producer and had become the Habs' best forward at both ends of the ice.

Because Pacioretty is a large man, he is often considered a power-forward, but he uses his size more for better position-ing and leverage than to run over the opposition. He is a smooth skater with good speed and a strong shot to match. He will also crash the net as needed, but his more noted skill is coming down the wing and making excellent plays with his drive on net. In the upcoming 2015–16 campaign, Pacioretty has to focus on staying

healthy (especially after an offseason training injury to his knee) and keeping his play consistent throughout the season and into the playoffs. If he can manage these intentions, he will surely continue to be considered one the best left-wingers in the NHL.

Drafted 22nd overall by the Montreal Canadiens in 2007

Scored a league-leading 11 game-winning goals in 2013–14

Tied for first place in the league with a plus-38 rating in 2014–15

Recorded 144 goals and 280 points in 399 career games

CAREER HIGHLIGHTS

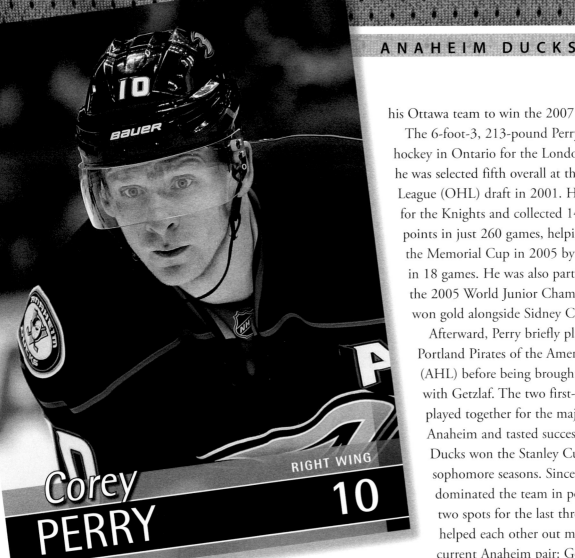

RIGHT WING

Corey PERRY 10

his Ottawa team to win the 2007 Stanley Cup.

The 6-foot-3, 213-pound Perry played junior hockey in Ontario for the London Knights, where he was selected fifth overall at the Ontario Hockey League (OHL) draft in 2001. He played four seasons for the Knights and collected 140 goals and 380 points in just 260 games, helping the team to win the Memorial Cup in 2005 by recording 38 points in 18 games. He was also part of Team Canada at the 2005 World Junior Championships, where he won gold alongside Sidney Crosby.

Afterward, Perry briefly played with the Portland Pirates of the American Hockey League (AHL) before being brought up to the big team with Getzlaf. The two first-round selections have played together for the majority of their time in Anaheim and tasted success early on when the Ducks won the Stanley Cup in the players' sophomore seasons. Since then, they have dominated the team in points, taking the top two spots for the last three seasons and have helped each other out more than any other current Anaheim pair: Getzlaf has assisted on 48.3 percent of Perry's regular goals and 58.1 percent of his playoff goals up to 2014–15.

Perry can be a little on the nasty side (with a franchise-leading 868 career penalty minutes to date) and seems to love getting under the skin of his opponents. Further, he is at his best when he gets in front of the net and awaits a pass or looks for a rebound. Perry's shot also has a lot of snap to it and he knows how to use it to his advantage (he has notched 27 or more goals seven times in his career thus far). Perry's best season came in 2010–11 when he scored a league-high 50 goals, earning him the Maurice "Rocket" Richard Trophy for top goal scorer, as well as the Hart Memorial Trophy as the NHL's MVP.

By the start of the 2014–15 season, the 2007 Stanley Cup–winning team was essentially gone, except for Perry, Getzlaf and defenseman Francois Beauchmin. The two forwards are now both 30 years old and the

Bryan Murray has been with the Ottawa Senators since 2007, as both head coach and general manager, but before moving north, he was employed as GM of the Mighty Ducks of Anaheim from 2002 to 2004. While in Anaheim, he played a big part in developing the team into Stanley Cup contenders. His work in the 2003 entry draft was the foundation the Ducks needed to eventually win the championship, and two of the first things on the agenda were selecting Ryan Getzlaf with the 19th overall pick and (after a deal with the Dallas Stars for a few draft choices) Corey Perry with the 28th overall pick. Murray thought a player like Perry would be an ideal fit at right wing, alongside Getzlaf at center, and just four years later, Murray was proven right as he watched his own draft picks run over chances of winning another championship are getting lower. The Ducks, however, did have another great regular season, finishing with 109 points, third place overall and first place in the Western Conference for the second consecutive year. They swept the Winnipeg Jets in the first round of the playoffs and only allowed one win for the Calgary Flames in Round 2. The Ducks just couldn't quite get themselves back to the Stanley Cup final, though, and the Chicago Blackhawks beat them in seven games. Perry still managed to have his best playoff run, with 18 points in 16 games, including two game-

winning goals, but if Anaheim wants to make it back to the finals in 2015–16 and claim the Cup for a second time, both Perry and Getzlaf need to take charge and lead their team back to glory.

Drafted 28th overall by the Anaheim Ducks in 2003

Led the league in game-winning goals in 2010–11

Named to the NHL's First All-Star Team twice

Led the league in even-strength goals in 2010–11 and 2013–14

Recorded 296 goals and 602 points in 722 career games

CAREER HIGHLIGHTS

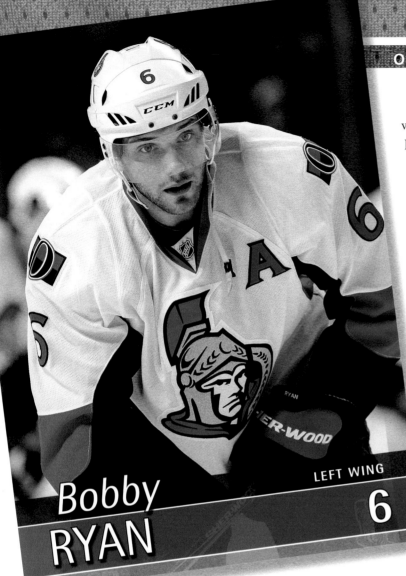

LEFT WING

Bobby RYAN

6

win at home forced a Game 5 back in Montreal. He scored twice against netminder Carey Price for a Senators victory, but that was the extent of his goal-scoring comeback, as Price shut out the Ottawa team in a 2–0 Montreal win to close out the best-of-seven series in six games.

The Ottawa club was fortunate to make the playoffs at all, considering they had fired their head coach Paul MacLean in December and looked to be well out of playoff contention. But then Andrew "The Hamburglar" Hammond took over the goalie crease in February and led the Senators on an epic run to the Eastern Conference's first wild-card spot. And while Ryan had his difficulties scoring, other forwards chipped in for a strong finish and he ended up with 36 assists and 54 points, which put him fourth on the team for the 2014–15 season.

Originally, it was because of Ryan's goal-scoring prowess that the Senators made a deal to acquire the native of Cherry Hill, New Jersey, for the 2013–14 season. Ottawa wanted some punch from a first-line winger and Ryan seemed like a perfect fit. In the end, Ryan's then–Anaheim Ducks were facing some salary-cap issues and reluctantly parted with their player who had scored 147 goals and 289 points in 378 games for the west-coast team. To seal the deal, Ottawa sent Anaheim two young prospects (Jakob Silfverberg and Stefan Noesen), as well as a 2014 first-round draft choice. It was clear how much the Senators wanted Ryan, and his first year in Ottawa was definitely successful, as he scored 23 times and added 25 assists in only 70 games (he finished the year on the injured list with a sports hernia).

The Senators were confident Ryan would recover well from surgery, but were not so sure if he would opt to continue his NHL career in Ottawa upon becoming a free agent. Many anticipated that Ryan would choose to go back home to play for the New Jersey Devils or Philadelphia Flyers, but he had come to embrace the Ottawa area, as well as his team, and he soon signed a

A s the opening round of the 2015 NHL playoffs was unfolding, the Ottawa Senators' star forward Bobby Ryan was as perplexed as anyone about his goal-scoring drought. At one point, Ryan had not managed to score in 16 consecutive games of the regular season and his 18-goal year (while playing in 78 contests) ended up being his worst since his 11-goal effort during the shortened lockout season of 2012–13. Ryan tried everything to get out of his funk, including watching a lot of video review. The Ottawa coaching staff also tried to keep Ryan as positive as possible, but the puck was simply not bouncing the right way for one of the most talented forwards in the NHL. Ryan did eventually find his groove again after the Senators were down 3–0 in playoff games to the Montreal Canadiens and a 1–0

seven-year deal worth just over $50 million. He also purchased a suite at Ottawa's home rink and now uses it to host local children and their families at every Senators home game.

Originally selected second overall by the Ducks in the 2005 entry draft (just after Sidney Crosby), the 6-foot-2, 207-pound Ryan has consistently shown he has incredibly soft hands coupled with a great desire to go to the net. These assets allow him to score picture-

CAREER HIGHLIGHTS

Drafted 2nd overall by the Anaheim Ducks in 2005

Nominated for the Calder Memorial Trophy in 2009

Recorded 77 points in 70 American Hockey League (AHL) games

Recorded 188 goals and 391 points in 526 career games

perfect goals and rack up points. He can also beat other players one-on-one, has a good shot that is concerning for goalies (especially with his expert deking abilities) and if opposing defensemen get on him, he uses his large frame to fight them off. There is no doubt that Ryan has the tools to play with intensity, and his spot on the Ottawa Senators' roster for the next seven years is the perfect place to show off those skills.

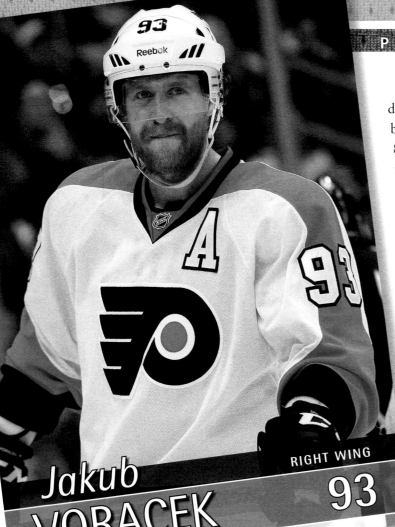

Jakub
VORACEK

RIGHT WING

93

didn't make the 2015 playoffs, Voracek still had a banner regular season that saw him hit a career-high 81 points, which was just one shy of allowing him to be a point-per-game player.

Expectations have always been high for the burly winger. Selected first overall by the Halifax Mooseheads of the Quebec Major Junior Hockey League (QMJHL) in the 2006 Canadian Hockey League (CHL) Import Draft, Voracek responded with 187 points in 112 games over two seasons. The QMJHL named Voracek to their All-Rookie team in 2007, in addition to handing him both the Michel Bergeron Trophy for being the top offensive rookie of the year and the RDS Cup that recognizes the best overall rookie.

Voracek also represented his country as a junior player, winning a bronze medal at the 2006 IIHF World U-18 Championships. He won his first international gold medal in 2010 when the Czech Republic beat Russia at the IIHF World Championships, and while he played for his country again in the 2014 Winter Olympics, his team lost to the United States in the quarterfinals.

Voracek didn't collect quite as much hardware in his three years with Columbus, but during his rookie season, he did help the Blue Jackets to make the playoffs for the first time in franchise history. In fact, he had the only assist on the club's first-ever playoff goal, but the NHL accolades really only started to roll in after his trade to the Flyers. Voracek signed a one-year contract with Philadelphia on July 1, 2011, which was the same day fellow Kladno native Jaromir Jagr also inked a deal with Philadelphia for one season. It didn't take long for Voracek to find his stride — he scored in his Flyers debut against the Boston Bruins, which put him on his way to an 18-goal season in 2011–12.

Philadelphia's hockey community also started to recognize Voracek's efforts, when in 2013 he received both the Pelle Lindbergh Memorial Trophy as the Flyers' most improved player and the Bobby Clarke Trophy that

It may have taken some time for Jakub Voracek to settle into the NHL, but since being traded by the Columbus Blue Jackets to the Philadelphia Flyers, he has continued to improve his game and become a prominent player. The right-winger from Kladno, Czech Republic, was selected seventh overall by the Blue Jackets at the 2007 NHL entry draft, and following a mediocre three seasons in Columbus was traded to the Flyers for center Jeff Carter in June 2011, along with a 2011 first-round draft pick (Sean Couturier) and a 2011 third-round selection.

The 6-foot-2, 214-pound Voracek only managed 134 points in 241 regular-season games with Columbus, but he has improved to 238 points in 290 regular-season games in Philadelphia. And, even though the Flyers

recognizes the team's most valuable player. Further, Voracek became so comfortable in Philadelphia that in 2012, he signed a four-year, $17-million contract extension to stay on with the team in the hope that he could fill the strong offensive hole left behind by Jagr's departure to the Dallas Stars. Voracek was put on a new line with Flyers stalwarts Claude Giroux and Scott Hartnell. He scored his first hat trick during the shortened 2012–13 season, which helped him earn the NHL First Star of the Week (for February 25, 2013) after he contributed 11 points in only four games.

Voracek is just 26 years old and still has a lot of hockey to play. More aggressive during the 2014–15 season, he registered a career-high 78 penalty minutes. This tougher disposition gave Voracek more room on the ice, which allowed him to record 81 points, tying him for fourth on the season with Alex Ovechkin.

CAREER HIGHLIGHTS

Voracek also finished second in assists with 59, which was just one behind Nicklas Backstrom. There is no doubt his game is maturing as he gets more comfortable in the NHL.

Voracek's name is now among the current NHL elite, and with the Flyers acquiring a new head coach in the relatively unknown Dave Hakstol, it will be up to players like him to lead the Philadelphia team back to the postseason in 2015–16.

YOUNG
GUNS

Alex
GALCHENYUK
CENTER/LEFT

Morgan
RIELLY
DEFENSE
44

Johnny
GAUDREAU
LEFT WING
13

Filip
FORSBERG   CENTER   9

price, so the deal was made. Two years later, Erat is with the Arizona Coyotes after bombing out in Washington, while Forsberg has become one of the best young players in the NHL.

After Forsberg was taken 11th overall by Washington in 2012, the team sent him back to his native Sweden to improve his play, and because of the trade to Nashville, never ended up playing a single game in a Capitals jersey. For the 2013–14 season, he started out in Nashville but spent most of his time with the Milwaukee Admirals of the American Hockey League (AHL), where he produced 34 points in 47 games. The Predators did call him up for 13 games and he scored his first NHL goal in his first game, a 3–2 win over the Minnesota Wild.

The start of the 2014-15 campaign saw Forsberg attend Nashville's training camp, determined to make the big team. The Predators kept the 20-year-old on the roster for the entire season and he responded beautifully with 63 points in 82 games. Forsberg was actually on pace to record a point per game, but he faltered after a great start, recording only 7 points in 15 games in March. Overall, the Predators had a great season with 47 wins and 104 points, which was enough to make the playoffs for the first time in three years. Forsberg's own impressive campaign included 26 goals (six of them game-winners) during the regular season and six points in six postseason games. It was helpful that the Predators had Peter Laviolette coaching the team for the first time since he stresses more offense that his predecessor, Barry Trotz, ever did.

Forsberg quickly showed that he has a good mind for the game and that his positioning is always strong. At 6-foot-1 and 200 pounds, Forsberg is not always the biggest player on the ice, but he shows no hesitation in throwing his weight around. Just ask Eric Boulton of the New York Islanders — he tried for a big hit on Forsberg, but bounced right off the solid forward. Forsberg will

Nashville Predators general manager David Poile admits to being disappointed in having to trade Martin Erat in 2013. The Czech-born right-winger had been a Predator since he was 20 years old and had appeared in 723 games for the team. Erat's time in Nashville had been perfect in many ways because he never complained or asked for an exorbitant salary, and he generated several seasons with 50-plus points. However, when the Predators were out of the playoff race in 2012–13 and the trade deadline was approaching, the Washington Capitals called about Erat's availability. The Washington club offered to exchange Erat for Filip Forsberg, a 2012 first-round draft choice. Poile couldn't turn down the offer that would give his team some much-needed young talent for a reasonable also block shots if necessary and was a plus-15 during the NHL regular season, which was good enough for third place among rookies in 2014–15. His balance in goals and assists further shows he is both competitive and a team player.

As the 2014–15 season wore on, Forsberg's offensive numbers didn't keep up to his original projections, but his 63-point, 82-game finish had him ahead of veteran Nashville centers like Mike Ribeiro and Mike Fisher. At one point, it even seemed a sure thing that Forsberg would at least be nominated for the Calder Memorial Trophy (especially after scoring 12 points in six consecutive games in November 2014), but when the nominees for the award were announced, Forsberg's name was missing. So, while he may not have officially won Rookie of the Year, he

was still the most successful rookie the Predators have had in their 16-season existence. He also led the team in 2014–15 in goals, points and power-play assists. Clearly, Forsberg has a promising career ahead of him on a very grateful Nashville Predators team.

Drafted 11th overall by the Washington Capitals in 2012

Participated in the 2015 All-Star Game as one of six rookies

Finished third in points for rookies in 2014–15

Recorded 27 goals and 69 points in 100 career games

CAREER HIGHLIGHTS

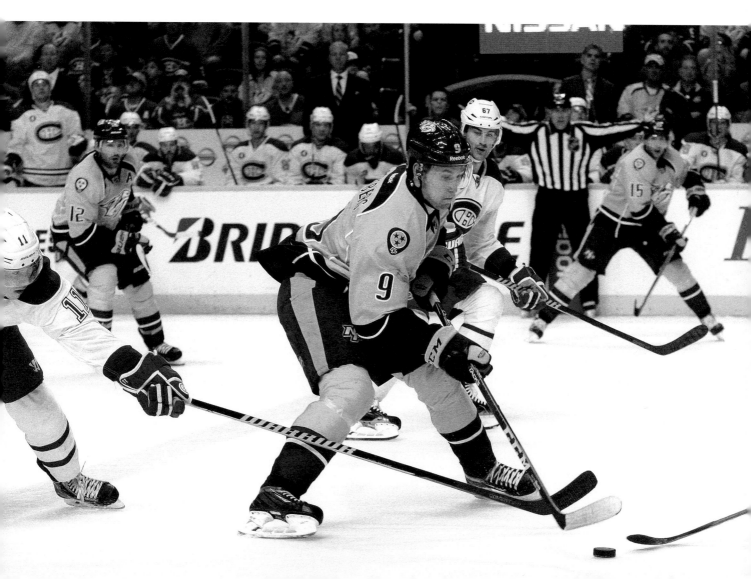

CENTER/LEFT WING

Alex
GALCHENYUK 27

forward who felt "unbelievable" to be chosen by such a historic franchise. He knew he had a lot to prove and didn't waste any time doing so.

Galchenyuk's path to the NHL was an unusual one, to say the least. He was born in Milwaukee, Wisconsin, but grew up in Russia before returning to North America to develop as a hockey player. Alex Galchenyuk Sr. was a Russian-born hockey player who played in his native country until he traveled to the United States to join the International Hockey League (IHL). He was playing for the Milwaukee Admirals in 1994 when his son was born, but when he realized that a minor pro career was all he was going to achieve, Alex Sr. decided to return to Europe with his family to compete there. Alex Jr. took to hockey while growing up, but there weren't enough European options to satisfy his needs, so he returned to North America to play in the juniors.

At the age of 15, he played for a junior team in the Chicago area and produced a whopping 87 points in just 38 games for the Chicago Young Americans. This impressive performance caught the eye of the Sarnia Sting, who took Galchenyuk on for the 2010–11 season. His next season was almost entirely wiped out by his knee injury, but the Canadiens' scouts had seen enough of Galchenyuk (83 points in 70 games over two seasons with the Sting) to make him their somewhat bold first round draft pick.

Instead of returning Galchenyuk to the juniors for at least one more year, the Canadiens decided to keep him on the big team once the NHL lockout was over in January 2013. Galchenyuk was playing back in Sarnia while the lockout was going on (recording 61 points in 33 games), but the Habs felt he was ready to try and help the team in Montreal that was eager to add a large forward to its roster. Galchenyuk ended up playing in all 48 games and scored nine goals, two of which were game-winners. His 18 assists tied him in sixth place on the team that season and he even led the

A lex Galchenyuk was believed to be one of the most talented players available at the 2012 entry draft. His 6-foot-1, 203-pound frame and incredible numbers for the Sarnia Sting in the Ontario Hockey League (OHL) made him a tantalizing prospect. The only problem was that the youngster had missed almost all of the 2011–12 season because of a serious knee injury. He had been productive the year before with 83 points in 68 games, but NHL teams are generally cautious about drafting players who have had knee issues. But, after the Edmonton Oilers selected Nail Yakupov first overall and the Columbus Blue Jackets took Ryan Murray second, the Montreal Canadiens stepped up to the podium to announce Galchenyuk's name. This moment meant a great deal to the strong

Habs with a plus-14 rating. Galchenyuk's second year saw him raise his point total to 31 and his maturity continued to grow as he became more comfortable playing in the NHL.

In 2014–15, Canadiens coach Michel Therrien decided to put Galchenyuk on the left wing rather than at center for most of the season. This was a smart move, as Galchenyuk had his best campaign yet, producing 20 goals and 46 points. He plays at his best when he is moving quickly and has shown some very soft hands when he gets in close to the

net. Galchenyuk tied with team leader Max Pacioretty for shooting percentage (12.3), yet had less ice time and fewer shots on goal, showing that his enthusiastic drives to the net are often successful.

At only 21 years old, Galchenyuk has plenty of time to further improve his game and the Montreal coaches will likely continue to give him room to show off his skills as he remains one of the most talented young players in the NHL right now.

CAREER HIGHLIGHTS

Drafted 3rd overall by the Montreal Canadiens in 2012

Named to OHL All-Rookie Team in 2011

Has 10 points in 22 playoff games

Recorded 42 goals and 104 points in 193 career games

LEFT WING

Johnny GAUDREAU 13

Gaudreau was born in Salem, New Jersey, and as a child grew up playing baseball, basketball, soccer and, of course, hockey. He loved sports but his father Guy also told him that he needed to work harder than everyone else because he was so much smaller. No stranger to hustle, Gaudreau racked up 72 points in 60 games for the Saints after playing high school hockey, where he scored 48 points in just 14 games. His hard work paid off and the Flames took notice.

By the 2011–12 season, Gaudreau was playing for the Boston College Eagles. He played there for his next three seasons and was outstanding in his final year, recording 80 points in 40 games. His success resulted in his win of the 2014 Hobey Baker Award that is given to the best player in U.S. collegiate hockey. It was also at Boston College that Gaudreau was given the moniker "Johnny Hockey" — a nickname so fitting that his agent has now registered it as a trademark.

As soon as his college career ended, Gaudreau signed a contract with the Flames and was in the Calgary lineup for the final game of the 2013–14 season. Not only was it his debut NHL hockey game, but he scored his first goal as well, which happened to be the only Flames point of the night.

Both the Flames coach Bob Hartley and general manager Brad Treliving were exicted about Gaudreau's skill level, but were unsure about whether he could handle the pace of multiple NHL games. Their concerns were genuine but misplaced because in 2014–15, Gaudreau went out and racked up 24 goals and 64 points in 80 games. If his size was going to be an issue, it certainly did not come up and the Flames were not about to waste a roster spot on a player who could not contribute on a nightly basis. Hartley was determined that the Flames were going to make the playoffs in 2015, and it would have been difficult to see Calgary in the postseason without Gaudreau's regular-season contribution. Among the Flames, he finished second in points, fifth in plus/minus, third in shots on goal

When former NHL player Jim Montgomery was coaching the Dubuque Fighting Saints of the United States Hockey League (USHL), he would often get asked about one of his smallest players. Montgomery would always answer the queries about Johnny Gaudreau by saying he wasn't sure if the 5-foot-9, 150-pound left-winger could play in the big-league circuit, but if he could adapt, then any team taking him would get a top-6 forward and power-play specialist. The Calgary Flames were one of the teams making inquiries about Gaudreau and they decided to take a chance on him by selecting him in the fourth round of the 2011 entry draft. It's still early in his career, but going by his rookie performance in 2014–15, the Calgary club should be glad they chose "Johnny Hockey."

and tied for first with 21 power-play points. He also contributed nine points in 11 playoff games as the Flames ousted the Vancouver Canucks in the opening round. Calgary faced the intimidating Anaheim Ducks in Round 2 but only managed to score one goal in the first two games while giving up nine. Determined to win on home ice, the Flames fought their way through Game 3, and with 20 seconds left in the third period, Johnny Hockey tied the game 3–3 to force overtime. The crowd went nuts and fed the Flames the energy they needed to win just over four minutes into extra time.

Commentators described Gaudreau as "deft, delicate, deadly," which is the exact combination most teams only dream of in a player.

And, judging by his performance, it's clear that the future of hockey in Calgary looks promising, especially with a player like Johnny Hockey on the roster.

Drafted 104st overall by the Calgary Flames in 2011

Led all rookies in assists in 2014–15 with 40

Named winner of the Hobey Baker Award in 2014

Nominated for the 2015 Calder Memorial Trophy

Recorded 25 goals and 65 points in 81 career games

CAREER HIGHLIGHTS

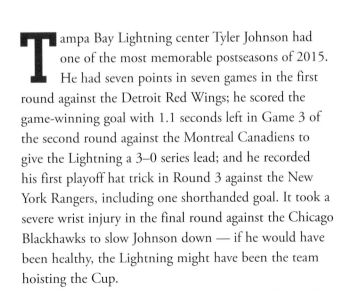

Tyler
JOHNSON

CENTER

9

instructor. Johnson took his lessons seriously and his superior skating skills were clearly evident, but he was so small that nobody believed he could play hockey at the higher levels. The Spokane Chiefs of the Western Hockey League (WHL) took a chance on him and in 2005 he was drafted to the league in the 11th round, but the team wasn't expecting much from the short center. They grossly underestimated Johnson, however, and in his first year in the WHL in 2007–08, he helped lead the Chiefs to a Memorial Cup victory. By his final season in Spokane in 2010–11, Johnson led the WHL in goals with 53 and finished the year with 115 points. Despite his impressive performances, every NHL team passed on drafting Johnson for three straight seasons until Tampa Bay finally signed him as a free agent in March 2011.

In 2011–12, he led the Norfolk Admirals of the American Hockey League (AHL) to their first-ever Calder Cup. Johnson had 14 points in 14 playoff games as the Admirals stormed through the postseason to take the championship. The team moved to Syracuse for the 2012–13 season and Johnson led the league in goals with 37. He also helped the Lightning that year with six points in 14 games before being promoted to their roster for the start of the 2013–14 campaign. He tied a franchise record for rookies with 24 goals and was a finalist for the Calder Memorial Trophy for recording 50 points in all 82 games. If that performance was not impressive enough, Johnson racked up 29 goals and 72 points in 2014–15, virtually erasing any lingering doubts about his ability to play in the NHL.

Johnson is listed at 5-foot-9 but he is a rather sturdy 182 pounds. He is not afraid to use his body to get to a loose puck and his speed is still his most valuable asset. Johnson has an accurate shot because he can pick deceptively difficult spots and get the puck through. He was put with Ondrej Palat and Nikita Kucherov to form the so-called "Triplets" line (a reference to the small size of

T ampa Bay Lightning center Tyler Johnson had one of the most memorable postseasons of 2015. He had seven points in seven games in the first round against the Detroit Red Wings; he scored the game-winning goal with 1.1 seconds left in Game 3 of the second round against the Montreal Canadiens to give the Lightning a 3–0 series lead; and he recorded his first playoff hat trick in Round 3 against the New York Rangers, including one shorthanded goal. It took a severe wrist injury in the final round against the Chicago Blackhawks to slow Johnson down — if he would have been healthy, the Lightning might have been the team hoisting the Cup.

A native of Spokane, Washington, Johnson learned to skate with his mother Debbie, who was a skating the three forwards), and the trio combined for a rating of plus-102, taking three of the four top spots in the league for the 2014–15 regular season. Johnson also led the 2015 playoffs in goals with 13, including four game-winners for the Lightning as they made it all the way to the Stanley Cup final for the first time since the club won the championship in 2004. The Blackhawks, however, were too good for the young team, winning the series in six games.

Johnson has barely made a dent in his NHL career but has already put his name in the Tampa Bay Lightning record books. He holds second place for a career rating of plus-59, seventh place for goals per game (0.32) and eighth place for points per game (0.74). He also won several awards

in the WHL and AHL, but has yet to win any in the NHL. At just 25 years old, however, he has plenty of time to add to his trophy case.

Gold-medal-winner with Team USA at the World Junior Championships in 2010

Part of the NHL First All-Rookie Team in 2013–14

Tied for first in the league in 2013–14 for shorthanded goals, with five

Recorded 56 goals and 128 points in 173 career games

CAREER HIGHLIGHTS

Nathan
MacKINNON 29
CENTER

the way to winning the Most Valuable Player award of the tournament.

The NHL draft wasn't the first time MacKinnon had been selected first overall. He had the same honor when the Baie-Comeau Drakkar took him at number one during the QMJHL draft of 2011 (about a month later his rights were traded to the Mooseheads). MacKinnon had been an impressive player in the minor leagues, recording 255 points over 85 games as a member of the Cole Harbour Red Wings. He then went on to board at the famous Shattuck-St. Mary's School in Minnesota — the same place where Sidney Crosby had played hockey. MacKinnon produced 101 points in his first year in Minnesota and 93 in his second. When he went back home to play for the Mooseheads, his regular-season totals included 63 goals and 153 points over two seasons. Because of this minor league success, there was little doubt that MacKinnon wouldn't make the Avalanche's roster on his first try.

Colorado had not been a very good team in the season prior to selecting MacKinnon — hence their winning of the lottery pick — so there was room on the roster for a young player like MacKinnon to make an impression. He got off to a great start in 2013–14, registering seven points in his first six NHL games. Roy used the youngster in nearly every situation — late in games when trailing and needing a goal; ahead and protecting a lead; the power play and the penalty kill. This gave MacKinnon a good grounding of what was required in the NHL.

MacKinnon responded well, with 24 goals and 39 assists for a rookie-leading 63 points in 2013–14 (eight of MacKinnon's goals were on the power play and five were game-winning tallies). His season was good enough to give him a landslide win in Calder Memorial Trophy voting, as the talented center received 130 first-place votes while the runner-up, Ondrej Palat of the Tampa Bay Lightning, had only five first-place votes. MacKinnon also finished second on his team with

When the Colorado Avalanche hired Patrick Roy as their head coach and vice president of hockey operations on May 23, 2013, the team knew someone was taking over who had very firm ideas about who he wanted on his hockey team. So when it came time for the Avalanche to make the first pick of the 2013 entry draft, Roy insisted that Halifax, Nova Scotia, native Nathan MacKinnon was the best choice. Roy was familiar with the 6-foot, 182-pound center since he had coached against MacKinnon's junior team, the Halifax Mooseheads, when both coach and player were part of the Quebec Major Junior Hockey League (QMJHL). In fact, MacKinnon had led his junior team to the Memorial Cup championship in 2013, where he had 33 points in 17 playoff games on a plus-20 rating, just one behind former Calder Trophy winner Gabriel Landeskog.

The Avalanche won 52 games in 2013–14 and recorded 112 points, making the playoffs for the first time since 2009–10. Despite losing a tough seven-game series to the Minnesota Wild, the opportunity for MacKinnon to get a taste of NHL playoff action so soon in his career was outstanding for his development — he even scored an overtime winner in the series.

The 2014–15 campaign was not nearly as good for the Colorado team that got off to a bad start and never really recovered. The Avalanche won only 39 games and missed the postseason while MacKinnon injured his foot in March, reducing his year to 64 games. He still, however, managed to produce 14 goals and 38 points, as well as play for Canada at the World Hockey Championships in Prague. In another dose of valuable experience, Team Canada won the tournament, with MacKinnon scoring four goals and five assists in 10 games.

A big, bright future is expected for MacKinnon, and with a young and talented Avalanche team, it will only be a matter of time until the club is once again a true contender for the Cup.

CAREER HIGHLIGHTS

Drafted 1st overall by the Colorado Avalanche in 2013

Recorded at least one point in 13 consecutive games as a rookie

Won the 2014 Calder Memorial Trophy as best rookie

Gold-medal-winner with Canada at the 2015 World Championships

Recorded 38 goals and 101 points in 146 career games

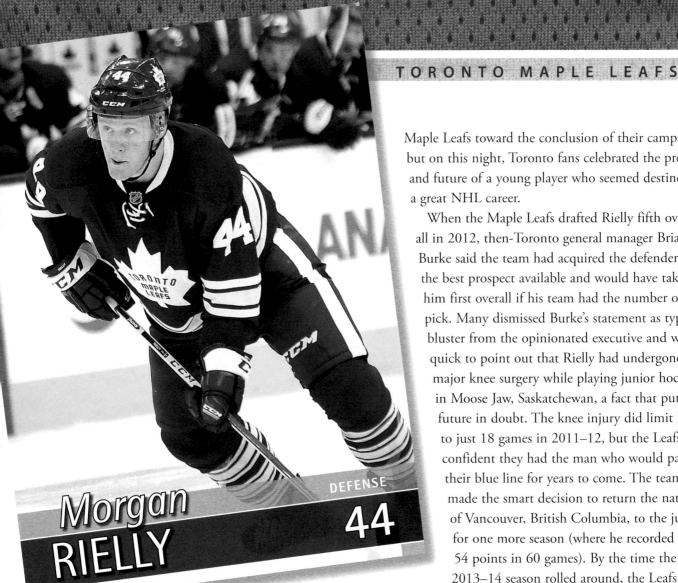

Morgan
RIELLY

DEFENSE

44

Toronto Maple Leafs defenseman Morgan Rielly had broken up the Edmonton Oilers' rush in his own end and taken the puck back up the ice, brushing past one defender as he started his journey to the opposite end. As he crossed the Edmonton blue line, Rielly cut into the middle of the ice, leaving an Oilers defenseman fishing for the puck. As the 21-year-old blue-liner approached the net, Rielly deftly kept the puck away from two other Edmonton defenders before roofing a beautiful shot over the glove side of goaltender Viktor Fasth, putting his drive just under the crossbar. It was a highlight-reel goal, and Rielly celebrated his marker with a whoop and a shout, helping the Maple Leafs to crush the young Edmonton team 5–1 late in the 2014–15 season. Not a lot had gone right for the

Maple Leafs toward the conclusion of their campaign, but on this night, Toronto fans celebrated the present and future of a young player who seemed destined for a great NHL career.

When the Maple Leafs drafted Rielly fifth overall in 2012, then-Toronto general manager Brian Burke said the team had acquired the defender as the best prospect available and would have taken him first overall if his team had the number one pick. Many dismissed Burke's statement as typical bluster from the opinionated executive and were quick to point out that Rielly had undergone major knee surgery while playing junior hockey in Moose Jaw, Saskatchewan, a fact that put his future in doubt. The knee injury did limit Rielly to just 18 games in 2011–12, but the Leafs were confident they had the man who would patrol their blue line for years to come. The team made the smart decision to return the native of Vancouver, British Columbia, to the juniors for one more season (where he recorded 54 points in 60 games). By the time the 2013–14 season rolled around, the Leafs had decided Rielly's spot was earned in the big leagues. He responded with an impressive 27-point season (placing him sixth amongst rookie defensemen) while playing in 73 games for the Maple Leafs, who faltered late in the season to miss the playoffs.

Rielly's main attribute is having a solid frame of 205 pounds and a height of 6-foot-1. He uses his strong legs to give him a mobile skating stride, and he can quickly get from one end of the rink to the other. He is great at gathering up the puck and taking it out of trouble — a skill the Maple Leafs' back line has lacked for many years. Rielly also passes well and crosses into the opposition's zone with confidence. In 2014–15, the second-year pro got his point total up to 29, including eight goals, which was an improvement over his rookie year that saw him score only two. But, despite his talent and consistent development, Rielly is still green and needs to improve his defensive play (he is a combined minus-30

over his two-year career). Offensively, he must also learn to hit the net more often, but if his first two NHL seasons are any indication of what Rielly can do, his raw skills won't stay that way for long.

When Randy Carlyle was coaching the Toronto club, Rielly often found himself critiqued by the former James Norris Memorial Trophy–winning defenseman. Rielly seemed to take it in stride, but when Carlyle was dismissed in January 2015, the blue-liner was tight-lipped when it came to praise for his former mentor. The new coaching staff gave Rielly more ice time so his offensive play increased as he recorded more points in the second half of the season.

Rielly is likely to be one of many young defenders the Maple Leafs will develop over the next two or three seasons. He has shown a maturity that is rare in players of his age and it is conceivable that he will become a leader of a new group of Maple Leafs who hope to be a consistent presence in the playoffs.

Drafted 5th overall by the Toronto Maple Leafs in 2012

Named to the Western Hockey League's (WHL's) Eastern Conference First All-Star Team in 2013

Played over 20 minutes per game in 2014–15

Recorded 10 goals and 56 points in 154 career games

CAREER HIGHLIGHTS

PROFILE INDEX

ACKNOWLEDGMENTS

I'd like to thank everyone at Firefly Books, especially Kara Steyn for her great work in helping put this book together. I'd also like to acknowledge Lionel Koffler, Michael Worek and Steve Cameron for their many years of great support for *Hockey Now!* Thanks to Kristen Lipscombe who provided research materials for three of the profiles in this book, as well as copyeditor Carla MacKay and designer Kimberley Young. As always, special thanks to my wife Maria and my son David for their encouragement and understanding.

Many media sources were consulted while writing this book, they are:

NEWSPAPERS
Toronto Star, Toronto Sun, Globe & Mail, New York Post, Sun Media newspapers from Toronto, Ottawa, Winnipeg, Edmonton and Calgary, *National Post, Montreal Gazette, Chicago Tribune, Dallas Morning News, Philadelphia Inquirer, San Jose Mercury News, Tampa Bay Tribune, USA Today* and any of their affiliated websites and links to other sources. Stories from the *Canadian Press* and the *Associated Press* that appeared in a vast number of newspapers were also frequently referred to in compiling the profiles.

MAGAZINES
Sports Illustrated, Sportsnet Magazine, The Hockey News, McKeen's Hockey Yearbook 2014–15, Maclean's, The Sports Forecaster NHL Preview 2014–15.

WEBSITES
The Fourth Period, The-Hockey-News.com, TSN.ca, Hockeybuzz.com, hockeyfights.com, hockeydb.com, Sportsnet.ca, Hockey-Reference.com, yahoo.com, Wikipedia.com, youtube.com as well as NHL.com and its network of websites.

RECORD BOOKS
NHL Official Guide and Record Book 2015, 2014–15 Media Guides for each NHL team.

TELEVISION
Hockey Night in Canada, the NHL and *That's Hockey* on TSN, as well as games broadcast on Sportsnet and NBC Sports Network.

RADIO
Games broadcast in Toronto and an assortment of interviews completed on *1050 AM* in Toronto (TSN radio) and on *FAN 590* in Toronto (Sportsnet radio).

BOOKS
Various issues of Paul Romanuk's *Hockey Superstars* (including 2014–15 issue), published by Scholastic Books.